First World War
and Army of Occupation
War Diary
France, Belgium and Germany

2 DIVISION
Divisional Troops
Royal Army Medical Corps
4 Field Ambulance
1 June 1915 - 31 July 1915

WO95/1336/6

The Naval & Military Press Ltd
www.nmarchive.com
Published in association with The National Archives

Published by

The Naval & Military Press Ltd

Unit 10 Ridgewood Industrial Park,

Uckfield, East Sussex,

TN22 5QE England

Tel: +44 (0) 1825 749494

www.naval-military-press.com

www.nmarchive.com

This diary has been reprinted in facsimile from the original. Any imperfections are inevitably reproduced and the quality may fall short of modern type and cartographic standards.

© **Crown Copyright**
Images reproduced by permission of The National Archives, London, England, 2015.

Contents

Document type	Place/Title	Date From	Date To
Miscellaneous	2nd Division 4th Field Ambulance Vol XI		
War Diary	Lapugnoy	01/06/1915	05/06/1915
Miscellaneous	No.4 Field Ambulance	01/06/1915	01/06/1915
Miscellaneous	No.4 Field Ambulance	02/06/1915	02/06/1915
Miscellaneous	No.4 Field Ambulance	03/06/1915	03/06/1915
Miscellaneous	No.4 Field Ambulance	04/06/1915	04/06/1915
Miscellaneous	No.4 Field Ambulance	05/06/1915	05/06/1915
War Diary	Lapugnoy	05/06/1915	06/06/1915
Miscellaneous	No.4 Field Ambulance	06/06/1915	06/06/1915
War Diary	Lapugnoy	07/06/1915	07/06/1915
Miscellaneous	No.4 Field Ambulance	07/06/1915	07/06/1915
War Diary	Lapugnoy	08/06/1915	09/06/1915
Miscellaneous	No.4 Field Ambulance	09/06/1915	09/06/1915
Miscellaneous	Lapugnoy	10/06/1915	10/06/1915
Miscellaneous	No.4 Field Ambulance	10/06/1915	10/06/1915
War Diary	Lapugnoy	11/06/1915	12/06/1915
Miscellaneous	No.4 Field Amb	11/06/1915	11/06/1915
Miscellaneous	Lapugnoy	12/06/1915	12/06/1915
Miscellaneous	No.4 Field Ambulance	12/06/1915	12/06/1915
Miscellaneous	Lapugnoy	13/06/1915	13/06/1915
Miscellaneous	No.4 Field Ambulance	13/06/1915	13/06/1915
War Diary	Lapugnoy	13/06/1915	15/06/1915
Miscellaneous	No.4 Field Ambce	14/06/1915	14/06/1915
Miscellaneous	No.4 Fd. Ambce	15/06/1915	15/06/1915
War Diary	Lapugnoy	16/06/1915	18/06/1915
Miscellaneous	No.4 Field Ambulance	16/06/1915	16/06/1915
Miscellaneous	No.4 Field Ambulance	17/06/1915	17/06/1915
Miscellaneous	No.4 Field Ambulance	18/06/1915	18/06/1915
War Diary	Lapugnoy	19/06/1915	20/06/1915
Miscellaneous	No.4 Field Ambce	19/04/1915	19/04/1915
Miscellaneous	No.4 Fd Ambce	20/06/1915	20/06/1915
War Diary	Lapugnoy	20/06/1915	21/06/1915
Miscellaneous	No.4 Field Ambulance	21/06/1915	21/06/1915
War Diary	Lapugnoy	22/06/1915	24/06/1915
War Diary	Fouquieres	24/06/1915	24/06/1915
War Diary	Lapugnoy and Fouquieres	24/06/1915	24/06/1915
Miscellaneous	No.4 Field Ambulance	22/06/1915	22/06/1915
Miscellaneous	No.4 Field Ambulance	24/06/1915	24/06/1915
Miscellaneous	Lapugnoy	24/06/1915	24/06/1915
War Diary	Fouquieres	24/06/1915	25/06/1915
Diagram etc	Diagram		
Miscellaneous	No.4 Field Ambulance	25/06/1915	25/06/1915
War Diary	Fouquieres	26/06/1915	28/06/1915
Miscellaneous	No.4 Field Ambulance	26/06/1915	26/06/1915
Miscellaneous	No.4 Field Ambulance	27/06/1915	27/06/1915
Miscellaneous	No.4 Field Ambulance	28/07/1915	28/07/1915
War Diary	Fouquieres	28/06/1915	28/06/1915
War Diary	Fouquieres Vendin-Les-Bethune	29/06/1915	29/06/1915
War Diary	Vendin-Les-Bethune	29/06/1915	29/06/1915
Diagram etc	Diagram		

Miscellaneous	No.4 Field Ambulance	29/06/1915	29/06/1915
War Diary	Vendin Les Bethune	30/06/1915	30/06/1915
Miscellaneous	No.4 Field Ambulance	30/06/1915	30/06/1915
Heading	2nd Division No.4 Field Ambulance Vol XII		
War Diary	Vendin	01/07/1915	06/07/1915
Miscellaneous	No.4 Field Ambulance	06/07/1915	06/07/1915
Miscellaneous	No.4 Field Ambulance	07/07/1915	07/07/1915
War Diary	Vendin	07/07/1915	10/07/1915
Miscellaneous	No.4 Field Ambulance	08/07/1915	08/07/1915
Miscellaneous	No.4 Field Ambulance	09/07/1915	09/07/1915
Miscellaneous	No.4 Field Ambulance	10/07/1915	10/07/1915
Miscellaneous	No.4 Field Ambulance	11/07/1915	11/07/1915
War Diary	Vendin	11/07/1915	12/07/1915
Miscellaneous	No.4 Field Ambulance	12/07/1915	12/07/1915
Miscellaneous	No.4 Field Ambulance	13/07/1915	13/07/1915
War Diary	Vendin	12/07/1915	12/07/1915
War Diary	Vendin & Bethune	13/07/1915	13/07/1915
War Diary	Bethune	14/07/1915	14/07/1915
Miscellaneous	No.4 Field Ambulance	14/07/1915	14/07/1915
Miscellaneous	No.4 Field Ambulance	15/07/1915	15/07/1915
War Diary	Bethune	14/07/1915	17/07/1915
Miscellaneous	No.4 Field Ambulance	16/07/1915	16/07/1915
Miscellaneous	No.4 Field Ambulance	17/07/1915	17/07/1915
Miscellaneous	No.4 Field Ambulance	18/07/1915	18/07/1915
War Diary	Bethune	18/07/1915	20/07/1915
Miscellaneous	No.4 Field Ambulance	19/07/1915	19/07/1915
Miscellaneous	No.4 Field Ambulance	20/07/1915	20/07/1915
Miscellaneous	No.4 Field Ambulance	21/07/1915	21/07/1915
War Diary	Bethune	21/07/1915	23/07/1915
Miscellaneous	No.4 Field Ambulance	22/07/1915	22/07/1915
Miscellaneous	No.4 Field Ambulance	23/07/1915	23/07/1915
Miscellaneous	No.4 Field Ambulance	24/07/1915	24/07/1915
War Diary	Bethune	24/07/1915	26/07/1915
Miscellaneous	No.4 Field Ambulance	25/07/1915	25/07/1915
Miscellaneous	No.4 Field Ambulance	26/07/1915	26/07/1915
Miscellaneous	No.4 Field Ambulance	27/07/1915	27/07/1915
War Diary	Bethune	26/07/1915	28/07/1915
Miscellaneous	No.4 Field Ambulance	28/07/1915	28/07/1915
War Diary	No. 4 Field Ambulance	29/07/1915	29/07/1915
War Diary	Bethune	29/07/1915	30/07/1915
Miscellaneous	No.4 Field Ambulance	30/07/1915	30/07/1915
War Diary	Bethune	31/07/1915	31/07/1915
Miscellaneous	No.4 Field Ambulance	02/07/1915	02/07/1915
Miscellaneous	No.4 Field Ambulance	03/07/1915	03/07/1915
Miscellaneous	No.4 Field Ambulance	04/07/1915	04/07/1915
Miscellaneous	No.4 Field Ambulance	31/07/1915	31/07/1915
Miscellaneous	No.4 Field Ambulance	05/07/1915	05/07/1915

121/5845

Summarised   131/5845

2nd Division

4th Field Ambulance

Vol XL

June 1915.
5

Army Form C. 2118.

WAR DIARY
or
INTELLIGENCE SUMMARY.

(Erase heading not required.)

Instructions regarding War Diaries and Intelligence Summaries are contained in F.S. Regs., Part II and the Staff Manual respectively. Title pages will be prepared in manuscript.

Hour, Date, Place	Summary of Events and Information	Remarks and references to Appendices
June 1st. 1915. LAPUGNOY.	Number of Casualties - Officers 1. Other Ranks. 30. Evacuated by No. 7. M.A.C. 3. Discharged to Convalescent Coy. nil	
June 2nd 1915. LAPUGNOY.	Number of Casualties - Officers Nil. Other Ranks. 23. Evacuated by No. 7 M.A.C. Officers 1. Other Ranks 10. D.M.S. 1st Army visited the Dressing Station	
June 3rd. 1915. LAPUGNOY.	Number of Casualties - Officers - nil. Other Ranks. 10 Evacuated by No. 7. M.A.C. 1. Discharged to Convalescent Coy. 9.	
June 4th. 1915. LAPUGNOY.	Number of Casualties 4 5. Evacuated by No. 7 M.A.C. 5 Discharged to Convalescent Coy. 2	
June 5th. 1915. LAPUGNOY.	Number of Casualties Officers 2. Other Ranks. 12. Evacuated by No. 7 M.A.C. 5. Discharged to Convalescent Camp 11. Duty. Officers 1.	

(73989) W4141—463. 400,000. 9/14. H.&J.Ltd. Forms/C. 2118/10.

No. 4 Field Ambce.

Sick and wounded admitted during 24 hours ended 9 am. 1/6/15.

2nd Divn	Officers		Other Rks.		
	Sick	Wound	Sick	Wound	
R.A.M.C. 5 F.A.			1	+	
1st Kings			3	+	
3rd Colds. Gds.			2		× 1 evac'd
1st Irish Gds.			5		
2nd Oxfords			2		
2nd Colds. Gds.			1		
2nd Gren. Gds.			4		
1st R. Berks	1		4		× 1 evac'd
2 S. Staffs			3		
5 Kings			1		
R.E. Sig Co.			1		
2nd Worces			1		
1st Queens			1		
1st Herts			1		× evac'd
	1	—	30		

Evac'd by M.A.C.
Other Rks. + 3

Admitted officers 1 — —
" Other Rks. 30 —
Evac'd officers — —
" Other Rks. 3 —
Remaining officers 1 —
" Other Rks. 27 —

Lieut. J.L. CARR, 1st R. Berks   N.Y.D.

P.A. Lloyd Jones
Capt. R.A.M.C.
OC. No 4 Fd. Ambce

No. 4 Field Ambulance

Sick & wounded admitted during
24 hours ended 9. am 2/9/39.

Unit and Div	Officers		Other Ranks		Remarks
	Sick	Wnd	Sick	Wnd	
1st Irish Gds.			3		To Light Duty
2nd Grenadier Gds.			1		2nd Colds. – 1
2nd Coldstream Gds.			2		3rd -do- – 1
3rd -do-			1		1st Irish – 1
2nd South Staffs			3		2nd Gren. – 1
5th Kings			3		2nd Sth Staffs – 1
1st Berks			2		5th Kings – 1
1st Kents			1		1st Berks – 1
1st Leicesters			2		R.E. H.Q. 6 Hv. Bde – 1
R.E. H.Q. 6th Hde			1		1st Leicesters – 2
R.T.A.			3		1 Queens – 1
2nd Ox & Bucks			1		2nd Ox & Bucks – 1
1st Queens			2		1st Kings – 1
					/13
Total			23		Remaining 10 Evac?

Evac. by M.A.C:
Officers 1
Other Rks. 10

Ret to Light Duty:
Other Rks. 13

	S	W
Admitted Officers		
Other Rks.	23	
Evac. Officers		
Other Rks.	23	
Remaining Officers		
Other Rks.		

P.H. Lord Jones
Capt. R. Amb.
O.C. No 4 F.d Amb.

No. 4 Field Ambulance

No. of sick & wounded admitted during 24 hours ended 9 am 3/6/15.

Unit - 2nd Div.	Officers		Other Rks	
	Sick	Wndd	Sick	Wndd
1st Irish Gds	.	.	2*	.
2nd Grenadier Gds.	.	.	1	.
3rd Coldstream Gds	.	.	1	.
1st Herts	.	.	1	.
2nd Worcesters	.	.	1	.
M. M. G. Sect.	.	.	2	.
1st Berks	.	.	2	.
Total	.	.	10	.

* One - 1st Irish Gds No. 3227
Pte RUAND disease I.C.T. wrist, evacuated sick, the remaining total 9. to Light Duty Section.

			S	W
Evac by M.A.C.	Admitted Officers		.	.
Other Rks. 1	" Other Rks.		10	.
Retd to Light Duty	Evacuated Officers		.	.
Other Rks. 9	" Other Rks.		10	.
	Remaining Officers		.	.
	" Other Rks.		.	.

A.D.M.S. 2nd Div
3/6/15

P. H. L. Boyd-Jones
Capt. R. Amb.
O.C. No. 4 Fd. Amb.

No. 4 Field Ambulance

Of sick & wounded admitted during 24 hours ended 9 a.m. 14/5/15.

Units 2 Div	Officers		Other Rks		Remarks
	Sick	Wdd	Sick	Wdd	
1st Irish Gds			5		2 Light Duty
2nd Gren Gds			8		1 Gren - 1
3rd Colds. Gds			3		1 Berks - 1
1st Herts			1		
R.E. 11th F.B.Coy			3		
R.A.M.C. (5 F.A.)			2		
2nd Worcesters			5		
R.E. 5th Fes Coy			1		
2nd H.L.I.			1		
~~2nd Grenadiers~~					
A.S.C. 2.D.S.C.			1		
2nd Ox Bucks			3		
1st Berks			3		
N.M.F.S.			1		
7th Kings			1		
2nd Innis Fus.			2		
5th Kings			2		
R.F.A. 17th Bty			1		
R.G.A. 35th Hvy			1		
20 London			1		
Total			45		

Evac by v.y.m.a.
 Other Rks - 5
Retd to light duty
 Other Rks - 3

		S	W
Admitted	Officers	.	.
	Other Rks	45	.
Evac	Officers	.	.
	Other Rks	7	.
Remaining	Officers	.	.
	Other Rks	38	.

A H Lloyd Jones
Capt R.A.M.C.
o/c No 4 Fld Amb

No. 4 Field Ambulance
No. of sick & wounded admitted during 24 hours ended 9 am 5/6/15.

Units - 2nd Div.	Officers		O. Rks		Remarks
	Sick	Wdd	Sick	Wdd	To Light Duty
1st Irish Gds	1	.	3	.	2 Grn. Gds - 1
2nd Colds. Gds.	.	.	1	.	Irish Gds - 3
1st. Herts.	.	.	2	.	R.E. (11th Fd Cy) - 2
R.F.a 2 D.a.C.	.	.	2	.	R. ame (5.F.a.) - 1
A.S.C. (3 Coy)	.	.	1	.	1 Berks - 1
1st Berks	1	.	.	.	2 Loyers - 1
2nd Worcesters	.	.	1	.	4 Kings - 1
2nd H.L.I.	.	.	1	.	M.M.G.S. - 1
2nd South Staffs.	.	.	1	.	To Duty 2 Colds - 1
Total	2	.	12	.	

Prevailing Disease — Influenza
No. admitted with Dropsy — Nil.

Evac. by M.a.C.
  Officers — Nil
  Other Ranks — 5
Rep. to Duty
  Officers — nil
  Other Rks — 1
Rep. to Light Duty
  Other Ranks — 11
Transfd to No. 6. F.a. — 1

			S	W
Admitted	Officers	2	.	
"	Other Rks	12	.	
Evacuated	Officers	.	.	
"	Other Rks	18	.	
Remaining	Officers	.	.	
"	Other Rks	31	.	

1st Irish Gds.
1st Berks

Officers Admitted
2nd/Lt. R.H. HEARD — N.Y.D.
—"— W. HILLIARD — N.Y.D.

P.H. Lloyd Jones
Capt R. Ame
O.C. No. 4 Field Amb.

A.D.M.S.
2nd Div.
5/6/15.

Army Form C. 2118.

WAR DIARY
or
INTELLIGENCE SUMMARY.
(Erase heading not required.)

Hour, Date, Place	Summary of Events and Information	Remarks and references to Appendices
6th June, 1915. LAPUGNOY.	The following order was received from A.D.M.S. 2nd Division — "O.C. No.4 Fd. Ambce. M.D. 780. 6th. 1. Send one half a bearer Sub Division today to ANNEQUIN to take over an Advanced Dressing Station now held by 1/1 London Field Ambulance at F.29.b.8.9. Personnel from this party will also take over an aid post at CAMBRIN A.26.a.2.9. 2. Sick and wounded will be sent from there & posts to your Hd. Qrs. LAPUGNOY. 3. Move to be completed by 5 p.m. (Signed) O. Severs Major R.A.M.C. for A.D.M.S. 2nd Divn. The following order was also received from A.D.M.S. 2nd Divn O.C. 4 F.A. M.D. 784 6th. You will take over tomorrow the Dressing Station at SAILLY-LA-BOURSE now held by a Fd. Ambce. of 47th Divn also from a cycle at Bde. Hd. Qrs. NOYELLES-LES-VERMELLES. Arrange details direct with O.C. the London Fd. Amb. Acknowledge and report when move completed. (Signed) M.P. Hall. Col. A.D.M.S.	D.M.S.

WAR DIARY
or
INTELLIGENCE SUMMARY.
(Erase heading not required.)

Army Form C. 2118.

Hour, Date, Place	Summary of Events and Information	Remarks and references to Appendices
6th June, 1915. LAPUGNOY. (Continued)	The following orders were issued to Capt. McCullagh R.A.M.C. No. 4 Co. Ambce. "Capt. Vincent McCullagh R.A.M.C. (S.R.) M.7. 6th. Half of the bearer S.D. of C Section will parade under you at 11 a.m. today. Destination ANNEQUIN. 1. Take over Advanced Dressing Station there now held by 6th London F.A. at F.29, 6.8.9. On arrival take over and post at CAMBRIN A.26.a.2.9 any personnel you consider adequate personnel for duty there. 2. Sick and wounded to be sent to 4 F.A. LAPUGNOY. The Scotch Cart and Maltese Cart should accompany you. Two Ambulance wagons will be sent to you later in the day. (Signed) P.A. Lloyd-Jones Capt. R.A.M.C. OC No.4 F.A. Capt. McCullagh, R.A.M.C. with half of the personnel of C Section Bearer Sub. Division proceeded to CAMBRIN and took up his positions on the East of Road in CAMBRIN. He relieved from the 4th London Field Ambulance. He did not take over the billets in ANNEQUIN. Accompanied by Capt. Byas and Capt. McCullagh I inspected VERMELLES with a view to finding a house	P.M.[?]

WAR DIARY
~~INTELLIGENCE~~ SUMMARY
(Erase heading not required.)

Army Form C. 2118.

Hour, Date, Place	Summary of Events and Information	Remarks and references to Appendices
Continued	for use as a collecting post. A suitable house was found just N. of Cross Roads towards W. axis of town at a point about 20 yards from the Cross roads on E. side of road leading N. I inspected the road leading towards the Regimental Aid post in front. I found that VERMELLES was a good central position for the collection of wounded from the Sub Divr line which escaped from LES BRIGUES in the North to LE RUTOIRE in the South.

I inspected the road which led from VERMELLES to SAILLY-LA-BOURSE and found is had a good surface for motors and was under cover from the enemy for the first mile.

I also inspected the buildings at SAILLY-LA-BOURSE to be handed over to us by the 4th. London F.A. and found that there were 130 beds in large clean school, and a large hut which has been erected in the school grounds.

There were also several rooms to be used as Dressing Rooms, Kitchens, R/c. A good billet was found for the officers. The men were bivouaced and the houses picketed in a piece.

Number of Casualties - Officers 1. Other Ranks. 13.
Discharged to light Duty. Convalescent Coy. 11.
Evacuated by No.7. M.A.C. 7 | PMG |

No. 4 Field Ambulance

No. of sick & wounded admitted and Transferred from No. 5 Field Amb. during 24 hrs ended 9 am 6/4/15.

Unit - 2nd Div.	Officers		Other Rks		Remarks
	Sick	Wded	Sick	Wded	
Transfers					To Light Duty:
1st Irish Gds			7	.	1 Irish — 1
3rd Colds Gds			2	.	1 Shew — 3
1st Herts			2	.	3 Colds — 1
R.G.A (2 Siege Bty)			1	.	1 Herts — 1
1st K.R.R			1	.	2 Worces — 1
R. amb (5 F.a)	1	.		.	2 Ox & Bks — 3
Total	1	.	13	.	2 Innis Fus — 1

Ordinary admissions   Nil

Evacd by No. 7 C.C.   Admitted   Officers — 1
  Other Ranks — 7   Other Ranks — 13
Retd to Light Duty   Evac'd   Officers   Nil
  Other Ranks — 11   Other Ranks 19
Transf'd to No. 6 F.a   Remaining   Officers — 3
  Other Ranks — 1   Other Ranks 25

Officers admitted.
R. amb. (5 Fa)   Lt. W. DUGUID   S.C.J. Foob

P. H. Lloyd Jones
Capt. R. amb
OC No. 4 Fd Amb

ADM.S.
2 Div. 6/4/15.

WAR DIARY
or
INTELLIGENCE SUMMARY.
(Erase heading not required.)

Army Form C. 2118.

Hour, Date, Place	Summary of Events and Information	Remarks and references to Appendices
7th June, 1915. LAPUGNOY.	Together with the Admiral and Brigr. I went to inspect the premises at SAILLY-LA-BOURSE. The Admiral agreed with me that the position at CAMBRIN and the divisional arrangements made by the London F.D. Ambce. should be discontinued and that the wounded should be collected to VERMELLES and from there taken to SAILLY-LA-BOURSE. The 4th Guards Brigade took over the Northern half of the line last night and the 6th. Infantry Brigade the Southern Half. Capt. Byas, R.A.M.C. with the rest of C. Section started for SAILLY-LA-BOURSE this afternoon taking with him his personnel and transport complete. Capt. McCullagh had orders to join him there and Lieut Andrews is also detailed for duty there. Capt. McCullagh and Lieut Andrews will sleep on alternate nights in Vermelles. Four Ambulance Wagons have been allotted to the Section at SAILLY-LA-BOURSE. Number of Casualties - Officers 3. Other Ranks 17. Evacuated by No. 7. M.A.C. 17. To Convalescent Coy. 9. Discharged to duty 2.	PMG.

WAR DIARY
or
INTELLIGENCE SUMMARY.

(Erase heading not required.)

Army Form C. 2118.

Hour, Date, Place	Summary of Events and Information	Remarks and references to Appendices
7th June, 1915. LAPUGNOY. (Continued)	The following order was received from Admin. 2nd Divn:— 1. Slight Sick and Wounded cases from the New 2nd Divn line will be sent to No. 4 Fd. Ambce. LAPUGNOY. 2. Sick and wounded of a more severe nature will be sent to No. 5 Fd. Ambce at ECOLE MATERNELLE, BETHUNE. 3. Local cases will be admitted to the nearest F.A. as before. 4. Scabies cases will be sent to No. 6 F.A. at MONT EVENIC. (Signed) O. Sevens, Major. for Admin. 2nd Divn	AAG.

No. 4 Field Ambulance

Nominal return numbers admitted & transferred from No. 8 Field Amb, during 24 hours ended 9 a.m. 7/6/15.

Units - 2nd Div	Officers		Other Ranks		Remarks
	Sick	Wd.	Sick	Wd.	
(Transfers)					To Duty
2nd S. Staff.	1		6		Hy. A.S.C. - 1
2nd Colds. Gds.			1		2 A.C. R.F.A. - 1
1st Divis.			1		
1st Herts			1		
R.E. 11 Fld Coy			1		To Light Duty
5th Kings			1		1 Irish - 5
1st Irish			1		1 Herts - 3
R.F.A. (2 Siege Bty)			1		Scores - 1
-do- (Gordon Irish)			1		
3 South Irish Horse			1		
Total			15		
(Admissions)					
R.A.M.C. No 7 F.A.			1		
2nd S. Staff	1				
5th Kings	1				
1st Herts	1		1		
R.F.C. (4-7 Bty)		1	1		
R.E. East Anglian					
Total	3	1	2		

Evac'd by No. 7 M.A.C.   Admitted Officers 3
Other Ranks - 17   " Other Rks 17
To Light Duty   Evac'd Officers N/L
Other Ranks - 9   " Other Rks 28
Ret'd to Duty   Remaining Officers 5
Other Ranks - 2   " Other Rks 15

Admitted Officers:
5th Kings   Lieut. R. BOWER   N.Y.D.
1st Herts   Capt. H. PAYLE
2nd Divn   "   G.L. BERRYMAN
R.E. (East Ang)   2/Lt. B.T. BRADDELL

7/6/15

P.A. Jordan
O.C. No. 4 F. Amb.

Army Form C. 2118.

WAR DIARY
or
INTELLIGENCE SUMMARY.
(Erase heading not required.)

Instructions regarding War Diaries and Intelligence Summaries are contained in F. S. Regs., Part II and the Staff Manual respectively. Title pages will be prepared in manuscript.

Hour, Date, Place	Summary of Events and Information	Remarks and references to Appendices
8th June, 1915 LA BUC NOY.	No. 255 Cpl. F Tophill, R.A.M.C. } To Duty with No 8 B.F.A. " 3165 - T Davies, R.A.M.C. } Lahore Divn. No. of Casualties - Officers - nil Other Rks. 16. Evacuated by No. 7. M.A.C. " 1 " " 4 Discharged to Convalescent Coy. 6.	PRG
9th June, 1915 LA BUC NOY.	Casualties admitted - Officers 2. Other Rks. 9. Evacuated by No. 7 M.A.C. Officers 1. Other Rks. 7. Discharged to Duty Officers 1. " " Convalescent Company 6.	

No. 4 Field Ambulance

No. of sick & wounded admitted & transferred from No. 5 Field Amb. during 24 hours ended 9.0 am 8/6/15.

Units. 2nd Div.	Officers		Other Rks.		Remarks.
	Sick	Wnded	Sick	Wnded	
Transfers:					To Light Duty
1st Irish Fus.	.	.	2	.	1 Irish – 1
2nd South Staff.	.	.	1	.	1 Fus. – 1
2nd Ox & Bucks	.	.	5	.	1 Hats – 1
2nd Worcesters	.	.	3	.	R. pnt(1.J.d) – 1
					2 Wor – 2
Total	.	.	11	.	
Admissions.					
2nd Trans. Sqn.	.	.	1	.	
R.G.A (11th Bty)	.	.	1	.	
A.S.C. 11th Coy	.	.	1	.	
" 6th "	.	.	1	.	
" 35th.	.	.	1	.	
Total	.	.	5	.	

Evac'd by No. 7. M.A.C.   Admitted   Officers   Nil
Officers   1   Other Rks. 16
Other Rks.   4   Evacuated   Officers   1
Ret'd to Light Duty   Other Rks. 10
Other Ranks – 6   Remaining   Officers   5
                                                Other Rks. 21

P.H. Hodgson
Capt. R.A.M.C.
O/C No. 4 Field Amb.

8/6/15.

No. 4 Field Ambulance.
No. of sick and wounded admitted during 24 hours ended 9 am. 9/6/15.

Unit. 2nd Div'n	Officers		Other Rks.		Remarks.
	Sick	Wnd.	Sick	Wnd.	
2nd Gren. Gds.		1			
2nd Colds.			1		
1st Herts.			4		
2nd H.L.I.	1				
5th. Kings.			2		
	1	1	7	—	
Other Div.					
19th London			1		
6th. London.			1		
Total.	—	—	2	—	

Evac'd J.M.AC.
  Officers — 1
  Other Rks — 7
Rev'd duty
  Officers — 1
  Other Rks. Nil
Rev'd Lt. Duty
  Other Rks. 6
Transf'd to No.5 FA
  Other Rks. 2

Prevailing Disease Nil
Admitted Nephritis 1.
Admitted Officers   Sick   Wnd.
                       1   1
  Other Rks.   9   —
Evacuated Officers   —   1
  Other Rks.   5   2
Remaining Officers   5   —
  Other Rks. 17   —

Lieut CORKRAN,   2nd Gren. Gds.   G.S.W. Femur.
Lieut H.W. WHITSON,   2nd H.L.I.   N.Y.D.

P.H. Lloyd Jones
Capt. RAMC
OC. No 4 FA.

Army Form C. 2118.

WAR DIARY
or
INTELLIGENCE SUMMARY.
(Erase heading not required.)

Instructions regarding War Diaries and Intelligence Summaries are contained in F.S. Regs, Part II. and the Staff Manual respectively. Title pages will be prepared in manuscript.

Hour, Date, Place	Summary of Events and Information	Remarks and references to Appendices
10th June, 1915 LAPUGNOY	I went to see the G.O.C. 6th. Infy. Bde. and visited the trenches with the Bde. major, 6th. Infy. Bde. and arranged the evacuation of the Southern line. For the present, extra dug outs for wounded at the site selected for the H.Q. of 2nd S. Staffs Regt. in the trenches are completed, the sick and wounded will be taken to the Farm at LE RUTOIRE at the Southern extremity of the line. After the 2nd S. Staffs. H.Q. is completed, the cases will remain in the dug outs for evacuation after dark. The regiments are to send a message to the collecting post at Vermelles at 9 p.m. every evening. Wagons will proceed along roads to collect wounded at 10 p.m. Special cases may be removed at the discretion of M.O. 4/c Regiments down the communication trenches to VERMELLES in day time. Three arrangements are made on account of the length of the communication trenches. Medical officers have authority to act for personnel from Bearer Sub. Division of C. Section to assist them in	OK19

WAR DIARY
or
INTELLIGENCE SUMMARY.
(Erase heading not required.)

Army Form C. 2118.

Instructions regarding War Diaries and Intelligence Summaries are contained in F.S. Regs., Part II. and the Staff Manual respectively. Title pages will be prepared in manuscript.

Hour, Date, Place	Summary of Events and Information	Remarks and references to Appendices
10th June, 1915. — LAPUGNOY. (continued)	Their duties at the Farm and Dug-outs. Evacuation from the Infty. Bde. area at Northern half of line is more difficult as there are no roads and the collection of wounded from here is being done in day time as well as night. The Collecting Post at CAMBRIN is being kept open. Number of Casualties Officers 1. Other Ranks 46. Evacuated by M.A.C. 3. Discharged to duty Officers 2. Other Ranks nil. " " Convalescent Coy. 7.	DAG.

No. 4 Field Ambulance.

N/o. of sick and wounded admitted by Units
during 24 hrs ended 9 a.m. 10/6/15.

Unit - 2nd Divn	Officers Sick	Officers Wnd	Other Rks Sick	Other Rks Wnd
2nd Gren. Gds.			1	
2nd Colds. Gds.			2	
3rd Colds. Gds.			6	
1st Irish Gds.			1	1
1st Herts			7	
1st R. Berks	1		3	
2nd S. Staffs			3	1
2th Kings			2	
1th Kings			5	
2nd H.L.I.			3	
R.E.A 2nd S.B.			1	
R.E. 2 Eng Co			1	
South. I. Hosp.			5	
Total	1	-	40	2
Other Divs				
R.F.A. 6th Lond.			1	1
Total	-	-	1	-

Evac'd J.M.A.C.
Officers. Nil
Other Rks - 3

Ret'd Duty
Officers 2
Other Rks Nil

Light Duty
Other Rks 8/5

No 5 Fd Amble
Other Rks - 7

Officers to Duty
2 Gren Gds
(Capt. Berryman)
1 Irish Gds.
(2.Lt. Heard)

To Light Duty
2nd Div. 2
2 S.Staffs 1
2 J. Gds. 1
A.S.C. 1
    8

No 5 F.H.
2 S. Staffs 2
3 Colds 2
1 Irish 1
1 Berks 1
5 Kings 1

		Sick	Wnd
Admitted	Officers	1	
	Other Rks	41	2
Evac'd	Officers	2	
	Other Rks	8	-
Rem'ing	Officers	8	
	Other Rks	46	

2nd. Lt. R. HAIGH, 1st R. Berks. - Self inf. fingers.

A.D.M.S. 2nd Divn

J.O.Kiffe
for Capt. R.A.M.C.
O.C. No. 4 F.A.

WAR DIARY or INTELLIGENCE SUMMARY.

Army Form C. 2118.

(Erase heading not required.)

Instructions regarding War Diaries and Intelligence Summaries are contained in F.S. Regs., Part II. and the Staff Manual respectively. Title pages will be prepared in manuscript.

Hour, Date, Place	Summary of Events and Information	Remarks and references to Appendices
11th June 1915. LAPUGNOY.	Number of Casualties - 27. Evacuated by No. 7 mV. A.C. 17. Discharged to duty 3. Convalescent Coy. 7. No. 6 Field Ambulance vacated the Chateau at MONT EVENIC and took over the schools at VERQUIN, E.29.C.	
12th June 1915. LAPUGNOY.	The O.M.S. 1st. Army visited the Dressing Station today. The following is an extract from 6th Infy. Bde. Orders No. 61, dealing with the evacuation of wounded in accordance with the arrangements made by the Commanding Officers, Bde. Major, and G.O.C. 6th Infy. Brigade. "1. The following arrangements have been made as regards the evacuation of wounded other than walking cases in section Y. (a) 41. The Regimental Aid Post at LE RUTOIRE FARM has good accommodation for wounded. The Medical Officer of the Battalion holding Y1. will send information every evening to the Medical Officer Y0. No. 4 Field Ambulance Dressing Station at VERMELLES as to the number spared for evacuation.	

No. 4 Field Amb.

No. Sick & wounded admitted during 24 hrs ended 9 a.m. 11/6/16.

Units. 2nd Div	Officers		Other Ranks		Remarks
	Sick	Wound	Sick	Wound	
3rd Colds. Gds			1	1	To Duty:-
2nd -do-			1	.	1 Irish Gds. — 1
2nd Gren. Gds.			2	.	2 Horses — 1
1st Irish Gds.			3	.	5th Irish Horse — 1
1st Herts			1	1	
2nd H.L.I.			2	.	To Light Duty
1st R. Berks.			1	3	1 Irish Gds — 1
2nd South Staffs.			1	3	3 Colds. — 1
1st Kings			1	1	1 Herts — 3
5th -do-			1	.	5 Kings — 1
7th -do-			2	.	R.F.A. — 1
R.F.A. 47th Bty.			1	.	
Total	.	.	17	8	Transfers to 5 F.A.
					2nd Gren. Gds. — 2
Other Divisions					1st Irish — 2
Royal Flying Corps	1	.			3 Colds. Gds. — 1
17th London R.F.A.	.	.	1	.	1 Herts — 1
South Irish Horse	.	.	1	.	2nd South Staff — 2
					1st Kings — 1
					1 Berks — 2
	1	.	2	.	7th Kings — 1
					12

Prevailing disease - Influenza
admitted nephritis - Nil.

Evacd by M.A.C.
Officers Nil
Other Ranks 17.
Retd to Duty
Officers Nil
Other Ranks 3
To Light Duty
Other Ranks 7
Transfers to No 5 — 12
" " " 6 (1 Irish Gds).

Royal Flying Corps.

		S	W
Admitted	Officers	.	.
	Other R.R.	19	8
Evacd.	Officers	.	.
— " —	Other Ranks	30	1
Remaining	Officers	6	.
— " —	Other Ranks	30	.

Admitted Officers
2nd Lt. E.E. Clarke S.C.I Jaw Smithies
P.A. Hopkins Capt. R. Aml.

Army Form C. 2118.

WAR DIARY
or
INTELLIGENCE SUMMARY.
(Erase heading not required.)

Hour, Date, Place	Summary of Events and Information	Remarks and references to Appendices
12th June, 1915 LAPUGNOY (Continued)	The latter will then send ambulances to LE RUTOIRE after dusk. (b) Y2 A Regimental Aid Post sufficient to accommodate 20 cases will eventually be established in dug-outs at the new Y2 H.Q. near the SHRINE. When this has been done, information as for Y1 will be given and wheeled stretchers will be sent along the HULLUCH Road after dusk. Pending the construction of the above Regimental Aid Post, LE RUTOIRE must be used by Y2 whenever possible. (c) Both sub-sections will do what they can by widening the conns of the communication trenches to facilitate the passage of wounded from the front line to the Regimental Aid Post. 2. The road from NOYELLES-LES-VERMELLES through L.11.b and L.12.a to VERMELLES is not to the used by wheeled traffic during the hours of daylight. (Signed) W. Kiley, B1. Major. Bde Major, 6th. Infy. Bde. Number of Casualties - Officers 2. other Rks. 38 Evacuated to M.A.C. Officer. – other Rks. 8 Discharged to Duty. Officers 1. other Rks. 5 Conveyances Company. 16.	

No. 4 Field Ambulance.

No. 8. sick and wounded admitted during 24 hours ended 9am. 12/6/15.

Unit and Service	Officers		Other Rks.	
	sick	wnd.	sick	wnd.
2nd Colds. Gds.				1
3rd " "			5	
1st Herts.			3	
RAMC (1st Herts)	1	–		
1st. R. Berks.			4	
7th. Kings.			4	2
5th "			2	–
1st "			2	–
1st. K.R.R.		1		
2nd. S. Staffs.	1		2	–
A.S.C. (M.T.) 47 N.			1	–
S. Irish Horse.			1	
R.E. Hd. Co.			1	
R.E. 2 Sig. Co.			1	
Total.	2	1	26	3
Other Divs				
A.S.C. 47 Div.			7	
R.F.A. 7th Lon.			1	
RAMC (6 Lon. F.A.)			1	
Total.	–	–	9	–

Officers to Duty
RAMC No 5 F.A.
Other Rks - Duty
3 Colds.   1.
7 Kings.   1.
1 R. Berks. 1. } 5
2 S. Staffs. 1.
2 H.L.I.   1.

Light Duty
2 Colds.   2.
R.E.   1.
2 Gren Gds. 1.
1 Kings   1.
7 Kings   1.
S.I.H.   1.   } 16
Irish Gds.   1.
1 Berks.   5.
2 S. Staffs. 1.
1 Queens   2.

Evacuated M.A.C.
  Officers Nil
  Other Rks. 8
To Duty.
  Officers 1.
  Other Rks. 5.
Light Duty.
  Other Rks. 16.

Prevailing Disease.
Admitted Nephritis
                    Sick Wnd
Admitted Officers   2   1
         Other Rks. 35   3
Evacuated Officers   1   –
         Other Rks. 29   –
Remng Officers   1   –
       Other Rks.   29   1.

Transferred from No.6 F.A. 4 sick.
Transferred to No 6 F.A. 1 "
Transferred to No 5 F.A.:-
   Officers 1 wounded
   Other Rks. 10 sick 2 wnd.

Lieut. S.H. CLARKE, RAMC 1st Herts.   N.Y.D.
Lieut Col. C.B. DAVIDSON, 2nd S. Staffs.   N.Y.D.

                                    P.H. Hoyt Jones
                                    Capt. RAMC.
A.D.M.S. 2nd Divn.   O.C. No 4 Fd. Ambce.

WAR DIARY
or
INTELLIGENCE SUMMARY
(Erase heading not required.)

Army Form C. 2118.

Hour, Date, Place	Summary of Events and Information	Remarks and references to Appendices
13th. June, 1915. LAPUGNOY.	I visited the trenches of the 4th Guards Bde. today and found arrangements for the evacuation of wounded very difficult owing to the length of the trenches. A dug-out had been made and the French evidence to accommodate 120 cases. The dug out is near to a road which could be used at night for taking the cases to VERMELLES. Near this dug-out there is also an old ruined house, of which all the walls have been knocked down and only the cellar left. It is proposed to use this cellar, connected by a trench with the trench in front of the dug-out. The walking cases and such cases as need immediate Hospital attention can be taken down the ordinary communication trench to CAMBRIN. A system of relays of stretcher bearers will be formed, and the event of an attack, at various intervals down this communication trench. A niche is made for the making of stretcher dug-outs ("Guy's Hospital") which runs from "Humanity Lane" Westwards to Slag Heap which is used as an observation post for Artillery to the S.W. of ANNEQUIN.	DMS.

Army Form C. 2118.

WAR DIARY
or
INTELLIGENCE SUMMARY.
(Erase heading not required.)

Instructions regarding War Diaries and Intelligence Summaries are contained in F.S. Regs., Part II. and the Staff Manual respectively. Title pages will be prepared in manuscript.

Hour, Date, Place	Summary of Events and Information	Remarks and references to Appendices
13th June, 1915 (Continued). LAPUGNOY.	There is a siding here and a yard used as a coal yard in times of peace. This hoped to be able to use this railway in the event of an attack for the transport of wounded. There is a plentiful supply of trucks. This would avoid the difficult transport down the long communication trench. (We were informed later that this railway would be kept for troops.) Unfortunately the railway, like the road to VERMELLES can only be used at night. There is a school in the village of ANNEQUIN close by the siding which might be used for about 80 patients. If the railway were used the patients would have to be evacuated along the LA-BASSEE – BETHUNE Road. For the present, the number of casualties is so small that they can easily be carried down the communication trench and evacuated to BETHUNE by motor ambulances with the sick. This is for the Battalion holding the Northern part of the line. The casualties of the Battalion holding the Southern part of the 4th. Infty. Bde. line can be evacuated in daylight to VERMELLES, by being carried down the	PK19

No. 4 Field Ambulance
Return of Sick and Wounded by Units, admitted during
24 hours ended 9 am. 13/6/15.

Unit 2nd Div.	Officers Sick	Officers Wnd.	Other Ranks Sick	Other Ranks Wnd.	
2nd Grenadier Gds.			1		To Light Duty
2nd Coldm. Gds.			5		
3rd Coldm. Gds.			4	1	
1st Irish Gds.			5		
10th Herts			3		
1st K.R.R.		1	1		
2nd S. Staffs			4		
1st Kings			1	1	
5th Kings			3	1	
7th Kings			2	1	
2nd H.L.I.			4		
R.E. 11th Co.			1		
R.F.A. 44 Brig.				1	
47th Bat.			1		
R.A.M.C. 2 F.A.			1		
Total		1	36	5	
Other Div.					
1st Queens			3		
R.F.A. Lond.			1		
Total			4		

Evacuated by M.A.C.
 Officers 1.
 Other Ranks Nil.
To Duty
 Officers Nil
 Other Ranks Nil.
Left Units
 Other Ranks 9.
Transferred 5 F.A. — 11 sick 4 wnd. 1 wnd. officer
Transferred 6 F.A. — 4 " — 4 "

2nd Lt. G.F. BEVAN, 1st K.R.R. Shell wnd. L.Side & R.Side.

Excluding Disease
Admitted Nephritis
                    Sick Wnd.
Admitted Officers   —   1
         Other Rks. 40   5
Evac'd   Officers   1   —
         Other Rks. —   —
Remaining Officers   6   1
          Other Rks.44   2

P.A. Lloyd Jones
Capt. R.A.M.C.
O.C. No.4 Fd. Amb.

A.D.M.S. 2nd Div.

WAR DIARY or INTELLIGENCE SUMMARY.

Army Form C. 2118.

(Erase heading not required.)

Instructions regarding War Diaries and Intelligence Summaries are contained in F.S. Regs., Part II. and the Staff Manual respectively. Title pages will be prepared in manuscript.

Hour, Date, Place	Summary of Events and Information	Remarks and references to Appendices
13th June, 1915. LAPUGNOY (continued).	Marched to the road and then by wheeled stretchers along the road to VERMELLES which is under cover. Number of Casualties - Officers 1. Other Ranks 45. Evacuated by No. 7 M.A.C. Officers 1. Discharged to Duty Nil. Convalescent Coy. 9.	
14th June, 1915 LAPUGNOY	Number of Casualties - Officers 1. Other Ranks 48. Evacuated by No. 7 M.A.C. Officers 1. Other Ranks 4. Discharged to Duty - Officers 1. Other Ranks 6. Convalescent Coy. 7.	
15th June, 1915 LAPUGNOY.	Number of Casualties - Officers 1 - Other Ranks 44. Evacuated by No. 7 M.A.C. Officers 1. Other Ranks 14. Discharged to Duty - Officers Nil. Other Ranks 2. Convalescent Coy. 11. No. 11613 Sgt. Major G. R. Morris, arrived from No 7 Field Ambulance, 3rd Division, for duty.	

No. 4 Fd. Amb.

Return of sick & wounded to Hosps. admitted during 24 hrs. ended 9 a.m. 14/6/15.

Unit & 2nd Divn.	Officers Sick	Officers Wnd.	Other Rks. Sick	Other Rks. Wnd.
2nd Gren. Gds.			3	—
2nd Colds.			2	—
3rd. Colds.			5	—
1st. Oxon.			2	6
1st. Herts.			5	—
1st. R. Berks			1	4
1st. K.R.R.			1	—
1st. Kings			2	1
5th. Kings			3	1
2nd. S. Staffs			2	—
7th. Kings			2	1
R.E. 5th. Fd. Co.			1	—
R.F.A. How. Batt.				1
R.A.M.C. 4 F.A.			1	—
R.A.M.C. 6 F.A. (as. 1 Herts)	1			
Total.	1	—	30	13

Other Divs.
1st Queens			2	—
R.F.A 4 7th. D.T.			1	—
" Low Dut.			2	—
			5	

Officers R. Duty
Fd. Berks. 1
F&S (A.R. Hoists) 1
Other R. Duty
1st R. Berks. 2
A.S.C. 4 Div. 1
R.F.A. " 1
2 Colds. Gds. 1
R.A.M.C.(7 Co 9) 1
                  6

Light Duty
A.S.C. 4 Div. 2
1 R. Berks. 1
R.A.M.C. 4 Dn. 1
S. Diths. 1
1 Queens 1
2nd. Colds. 1
                  7

Wnd's mate
Officers 1.
Other Rks. 4.
Duties
Officers 1.
Other Rks. 6.
Light Duty
Other Rks. 7.
Trans. 5 F.A.
  Other Rks. 9 sick 9 wnd
Trans 6 F.A.
  Other Rks. 2 sick.

Prevailing Disease
Acute Nephritis
                    Sick Wnd.
Admitted Officers   1   —
         Other Rks. 35   13
Trans'd Officers   1   —
         Other Rks. 4   —
Remng. Officers   5   —
         Other Rks. 51   6

Lieut G.A.C. MITCHELL, R.A.M.C. 6 F.A. (a. Hosp). 1 act. Reks. 13 ?
H.Q.M.S. 2nd Div
   14/6/15.
                                P.K. C... Jones
                                Capt. R.A.M.C.
                                O.C. No. 4 F.A.

No. 4 F.A. Antica.

Sick and wounded admitted by Units, during 24 hours ended 9 a.m. 15/6/15.

Unit 2nd Div.	Officers Sick	Officers Wnd	Other Rks. Sick	Other Rks. Wnd		
2nd Innis. Fus.	1		4		To duty	
2nd Colds.			1		7 A.M.C.	1.
1st Irish			8	2	47 Div Tn.	1.
3rd Colds.			-	5	To Con. Coy.	
1st Herts.			6	1	R.F.A. 17 Bde.	1.
1st Kings			1	1	1 Queens	1.
5th "			1		R.A.M.C. 4 F.A.	1.
7th Kings			5		A.S.C. 4 F.A.	1.
1st K.R.R.			1	-	R.F.A. 11 Bde.	1.
2nd S. Staff.			1	-	1 I. Fus.	1.
R.F.A. 36 Bde.			1	-	2 S. Staff.	1.
R.E. 11 Fd. Co.			-	7	2 Colds.	1.
A.S.C. 2 D.S.C.			1	-	1 Herts.	1.
1st K.R.R.			1	-	3 Colds.	2
Total	1	-	25	16		11
Other Div:						
1st Cameron				3		
Total			-	3		

Evac'd M.A.C.
Officers 1.
Other Rks. 14.
To Duty
Officers nil.
Other Rks. 2.
Const. Camp.
Other Rks. 14.

Trans. 5 F.A. 8 sick 14 wnd.
Trans. 6 F.A. 1 sick.

Prevailing Diseases –
Admitted Reports.
                    Sick Wnd.
Admitted Officers   1   -
          Other Rks. 25   19.
Evac'd   Officers   1
          Other Rks. 14   -
Remng   Officers
         Other Rks. 29   11

2nd Lt. J.N. BUCHANAN, 2nd Innis. Fus. Sun Fever.

P.H. Lloyd Jones
Capt. R.A.M.C.
O.C. No 4 F.A.

A.D.M.S. 2nd Div.

Army Form C. 2118.

WAR DIARY
or
~~INTELLIGENCE~~ SUMMARY.
(Erase heading not required.)

Instructions regarding War Diaries and Intelligence Summaries are contained in F.S. Regs., Part II. and the Staff Manual respectively. Title pages will be prepared in manuscript.

Hour, Date, Place	Summary of Events and Information	Remarks and references to Appendices
16th June, 1915. LAPUGNOY	Number of Casualties - Officers Nil. Other Ranks 47. Evacuated by No. 7 M.A.C. Officers Nil. - " - 9. Discharged to Duty. Officers 1 Other Rks. 7. " . Convalescent Coy. 13.	
17th June, 1915. LAPUGNOY	Number of Casualties - Officers 1 - Other Rks. 48. Evacuated by No. 7 M.A.C. " Nil. " 3. Discharged to Duty " Nil. " 1. " Conv. Coy. " Nil. " 11.	A.H.S.
18th June, 1915. LAPUGNOY	Number of Casualties Officers 2 Other Rks. 35. Evacuated by No. 7 M.A.C. Officers Nil Other Rks. 7. Discharged to Duty " 1 " 17. " . Convalescent Coy. 9	

No. 4 Field Ambulance

Sick and wounded admitted, by units, during 24 hours ended 9am. 16/6/15

2nd Divn Unit.	Officers sick wnd	Other Rks. sick wnd	
2nd Gren. Gds.		3 2	Officers to Duty
2nd Colds. Gds.		2 2	1st Herts. 1.
3rd Colds. Gds.		3 –	(Capt. H. Sawle)
1st Irish. Gds.		4 1	Other Rks Duty
1st He.Ls.		8 –	5 Kings 1.
1st K.R.R.		1 –	RAMC. 6 F.A. 1. } 7
1st Kings		1 –	7th Kings 5.
7th "		4 –	Conv. Coy.
1st R. Berks.		3 –	6 Lon. R.F.A. 2.
5th K.R.R.		1 –	Irish. Gds. 3.
2nd H.L.I.		4 –	3 Colds. 1. } 13.
R.G.A. 6th Batt.		1 –	1 Herts. 2.
R.E. 11th Fd. Co.		– 1	1 R. Berks. 3.
Total.		35 6	R.E. 11 Fd Co. 2.

Other Dvs.
1st Queens.		4 –	
R.F.A. bn. Lond		1 –	
A.S.C. Rhead. }		1 –	
Labor Co. }			
		6 –	

Evac'd M.A.C.
Officers – Nil
Other Rks – 9.
To Duty
Officers   1
Other Rks. 7.
Conv. Company.
Other Rks. – 13.
No 5 Fd. Amb. 3 sick 6 wnd.
No 6 Fd. Amb. 5 sick.

Cases Remne. 6.
	sick wnd
Remnd officers	– –
Other Rks.	41 6
Evac'd officers	– –
Other Rks.	9 –
Remng officers	4 –
Other Rks.	47 7

P.H. Lloyd Jones
Capt. RAMC
O.C. No.4 Fd. Amb.

A.D.M.S. 2nd Divn

No. 4 Field Ambulance

Sick and wounded admitted, by units, during 24 hours ended 9 am. 17/6/15.

Unit and Div.	Officers Sick	Officers Wnd.	Other Rks Sick	Other Rks Wnd.	To Duty	
2nd Gren. Gds.			2	2	1st Herts.	1.
2nd Colds. Gds.			2	-	Corr. Coy.	
3rd Colds.			6	-	7th Kings.	2.
1st Irish			2	-	2nd H.L.I.	1.
1st Herts.			7	-	3rd Colds.	1.
1st R. Berks.			1	-	1 Queens.	1.
2nd S. Staffs.			8	-	2nd Ox.	1.
1st Kings.			-	1	2 Gren Gds.	2.
5th "			2	-	1 R. Berks.	1.
Renn R?			-	-	R.E. 11 Co.	2
2nd Worcs.			-	2		11
2nd H.L.I.			1	-		
9th H.L.I.			4	-		
R.E. 5th 7 Co	1					
R.7A 36 Bde.				1		
Total.	1	-	35	6		

Other Divs.

1st Queens.			5	-	
1st Northants.			-	1	
A.S.C. 44th D.T.			1		
Total	-	-	6	1	

Evac'd M.A.C.
Officers Nil
Other Rks. 3

Ret'd Duty
Officers Nil
Other Rks. 1

Conv. Camp.
Other Ranks. 11

Trans 5 F.A. 12 sick 7 wnd.
Trans 6 F.A. 5 sick - wnd.

Scabies 5.

	Sick	Wnd
Admitted Officers	1	-
" Other Rks.	41	7
Evac'd Officers	-	-
" Other Rks.	5	-
Remaing Officers	-	-
Other Rks.	57	4

2nd Lt. H.F.G. GREENWOOD. R.E. 57 Co. Influenza

A.D.M.S. 2nd Divn

P.R. Ll?d Jones.
Capt. RAMC
O.C. No.4 F. Amb.

No. 4 Field Ambulance.

Sick and Wounded, by Units, admitted during 24 hrs.
ended 9 a.m. 18/6/15.

Unit and O.W.	Officers		Other Rks.	
	Sick	Wond	Sick	Wond
2nd Gren. Gds.			2	—
3rd Colds. Gds.			1	2
1st. Irish Gds.		1	—	8
1st. Herts			3	—
2nd Oxfords.			3	—
2nd H.L.I.			1	—
2nd Worces.			—	1
5th Kings.			1	—
1st K.R.R.	1	—	1	—
R.E. 11th. Co.			1	—
R.F.A. 47th. Bat.			1	—
36 Bde.			1	—
" 1st . Bde.			1	—
R.G.A 5 Sge Batt			1	—
9 "			1	—
R.F.A. 7 Fd. Batt.			1	—
A.S.C. 2nd Div.			2	—
Total	1	—	21	11

Other Divs.
| 1st. Queens. | | | 8 | — |
| Total | — | — | 3 | — |

Evac'd M.A.C.
Officers. nil
Other Rks. 7.
To Duty
Officers 1.
Other Rks. 19.
Conv. Coy.
Other Rks. 9.
No. 5 Fd. Amble { 1 Offrs.
{ 5 sick ½ wond.

Officers Duty
2nd H.L.I. 1.
(Lt. H. W. Whelan)
Other Rks. Duty
5th Kings 2.
1st Herts. 4.
2. H.L.I. 1.
3 Colds. 1.
R.F.A. 47 Bat. 1.
                9

Conv. Coy.
3rd Colds 2.
2. Gren Gds. 1.
1 R. Berks. 1.
5 Kings. 1.
1 Queens. 1.
R.F.A. 11 Bat. 1.
A.S.C.Z.A.S.C. 1.
R.F.A 47 Batt 1
                9

	Sick	Wond
Admitted Officers	1	1
" Other Rks.	24	11
Evac'd Officers	—	—
" Other Rks	nil	—
Remaining Officers		5
" Other Rks.	54	3

2nd Lt. L. S. STRAKER, 1st Irish Gds. Wound Concussion
Lieut. D. G. WIGAN, 1st K.R.R. Neurasthenia.

[signature]
Capt. RAMC.
O.C. No. 4 F.A.

Admd. 2nd Div.
18/6/15.

Army Form C. 2118.

WAR DIARY
or
INTELLIGENCE SUMMARY.
(Erase heading not required.)

Instructions regarding War Diaries and Intelligence
Summaries are contained in F.S. Regs., Part II.
and the Staff Manual respectively. Title pages
will be prepared in manuscript.

Hour, Date, Place	Summary of Events and Information	Remarks and references to Appendices
19th June 1915. LA PUGNOY.	A Medical Board on Lieut. C.E.W. BIRKETT, 2nd Somerset L.I. (S.R.) attached 1st K.R.R., a candidate for a commission in the Regular Forces. The officer was found fit. President. Officer Commanding. Members { Capt. J.J. O'Keefe, R.A.M.C. { Lieut. R.H. Murphy, R.A.M.C. Number of Casualties. Officers. 1. Other Ranks 8. Evacuated by No. 7. M.A.C. Officers 2. Other Ranks 6. Discharged to Duty Officer 1. Other Ranks 7. Convalescents Company 7.	PMQ
20th June, 1915. LA PUGNOY.	Visited the Advanced Dressing Stations at SAILLY-LA-BOURSE in company with the Sgt. Major. Inspected the Advanced Dressing Station Sanitary arrangements. Latrine Buckets in use there. 12 men were sent up to O.C. C. Section to keep with the digging at VERMELLES. Inspected VERMELLES Collecting Post and found that great progress had been made in preparing the cellars under the Château for the reception of wounded. I also inspected the "Wheeled Stretcher Track."	

No. 4 Field Ambce.
Sick and Wounded admitted 24 hrs ended
9 am. 19/10/15.

Unit. 2nd Div.	Officers Sick	Wnd.	Other Rks Sick	Wnd.
2nd Colds. Gds.			1	-
3rd " "			-	3
1st Herts.			1	-
2nd Worcs.			1	-
Total	-	-	3	3
Other Divs.				
1st Queens			2	-
6th London	1	-	-	-
	1	-	2	-

Officer Duty
2. S. Staffs.
Lt. Col. C. R. Davidson
Other Rks. Duty
1st Herts.   3.
Ad. C. 2 Div.   2.
R.S. 11 Co.   1.
3 Colds.   1.
Conv. Coy.
(See below)

Evac'd M.Ac.
Officers 2
Other Rks. 10
Duty
Officers. 1
Other Rks. 7
Con. Coy. ?
Other Rks. 17
No. 5 Fd. Amb. 3 sick. 3 wnd.

	Sick	Wnd
Admitted Officers	1	-
Other Rks.	5	3
Evac'd Officers	2	-
Other Rks.	6	-
Remaing Officers	3	-
Other Rks.	27	2

2nd Lt. H. B. WELLS, { R.F.A. {6th London. Periostitis

Convalescent Coy
1st Irish Gds. 1.
2. K.R.R.   2.
1 Herts.   5.
1 Queens   2.
2 Gren. Gds.   1.
3 Colds.   1.
1 R. Berks.   1.
R.G.A.   1.
2 Colds.   1.
5 Kings   2.
Total   17.

Trans. No. 5 Fd. Amb.

	Officers		Other Rks	
	S.	W.	S.	W.
3rd Colds.	-	-	-	3.
1 Herts.	-	-	1	-
2 Colds.	-	-	1	-
2 Worces.	-	-	1	-
Total	-	-	3	3

P. A. Lloyd Jones
Capt. R.A.M.C.
O.C. No 4 F.A.

A.D.M.S. 2nd Divn

No. 4 FD. Ambce.

Sick and wounded, by Units, admitted during 24 hrs ended 9 a.m. 20/6/15.

Unit - 2nd Div	Officers		Other Rks.	
	Sick	Wnd.	Sick	Wnd.
3rd Colds. Gds.	-	-	-	1
1st Irish Gds.	1	-	8	-
1st K.R.R.	-	-	1	-
2nd H.L.I.	-	-	6	-
9th	-	-	1	-
2 Worces.	-	-	1	1
R.F.N.	-	-	1	-
Total.	1	-	18	2

Evac'd M.N.C.
Officers -
Other Rks. 5.
Duty
Officers -
Other Rks. 1
Con. Coy.
Other Rks. 7.
Trans. 5 FD. Amb. 2 sick 2 wnd.

To Duty.
1st Queens 1.
Con. Coy.
2 H.L.I. 2.
1 Queens. 2.
1 R. Berks. 2.
A.S.C. 1
  7

Cases Dentine 7.

	Sick	Wnd.
Admitted Officers	1	-
Other Rks.	18	2
Evac'd Officers	-	-
Other Rks.	5	-
Remng. Officers	4	-
Other Rks.	30	2

2nd Lt. T. ROBYNS, 1st Irish Gds. Appendicitis.

Trans. No. 5 FD. Ambce.

	Sick	Wnd.
3rd Colds.	-	1
9 H.L.I.	1	-
2 Worces.	1	1
	2	2

P. H. Lloyd Jones
Capt. R.A.M.C.
O.C. No. 4 FD. Am.

A.D.M.S. 2nd Divn
20/6/15.

WAR DIARY
or
INTELLIGENCE SUMMARY.

(Erase heading not required.)

Army Form C. 2118.

Hour, Date, Place	Summary of Events and Information	Remarks and references to Appendices
20th June, 1915. LA PUGNOY.	I decided to evacuate cases from the Battalion on the left of 5th. Infty. Bde. i.e. from Y.2 (Trench map) and cases from B.1 (Right of 4th. Guards Brigade) by this route in the day time. Inspected CAMBRIN collecting post and found all satisfactory. Number of Casualties - Officers 1. Other Ranks 20. Evacuated by No.7 M.A.C. " Nil " " 5. Discharged to Duty " Nil " " 1. " Convales. Coy. " Nil " " 7.	PKY
21st June, 1915. LA PUGNOY.	Twelve men from B Section proceeded to O.C. Sections at SAILLY-LA-BOURSE for the purpose of assisting in digging work in the neighbourhood of VERMELLES. These men are to return immediately on the completion of duty. Special orders were issued to O.C. Sections to detail Special orders as tents pitched. Number of Casualties - Officers 1. Other Ranks 18. Evacuated by No.7 M.A.C. " 1 " " 6. Discharged to Duty " Nil " " 12. " Convalescent Company " " " 8.	

No. 4 Field Ambulance

Sick and Wounded admitted by Units during 24 hours ending 9 a.m. 21/6/15

2nd Div. Unit	Officers Sick	Officers Wnd	Other Rks. Sick	Other Rks. Wnd		
2nd Gren. Gds.			1	-	To Duty	
2nd Colds.	1	-	3	-	2nd Colds. Gds.	2
3rd "	1	-	1	-	3rd " "	1
1st Irish	-	-	6	1	1st Irish "	6
1st Herts	-	-	2	-	2nd. A.L.I.	1
2nd Oxfds.	-	-	3	-	R.F.A. 7 Batt.	1
1 R Berks	-	-	1	-	2nd Gren. Gds.	1
2 Worcs.	-	-	1	-		12
San. Sec. 2 Div.	-	-	-	1		
Total	1	-	17	1	Influenza 6.	

	Sick	Wnd
Admitted Officers	1	-
Other Rks.	17	1
Evac. Officers	-	-
Other Rks.	6	-
Remng Officers	4	-
Other Rks.	19	2

Evac. M.A.C.
Officers 0
Other Rks. 6
To Duty
Officers Nil
Other Rks. 12
Conv. Coy.
Other Rks. 8.
Trans. 5 Fd. Amb. 2 sick 1 wnd.

2nd Lt. A. J. H. SMITH, 2nd Colds. Gds. N.Y.D. chill.

To Con. Coy		Trans. 5 Fd. Amb.	Sick	Wnd
1st R Berks	2	2nd Worcs.	1	-
3rd Colds. Gds.	1	1st Hertons	1	-
1st Queens	1	San Sec 2 Div	-	1
R.F.A. 36 Batt.	1		2	1
2 Gren. Gds.	2			
1st Irish	1			
	8			

ADMS 2nd Div.
21/6/15.

Capt. RAMC
OC. No. 4 F.A.

Army Form C. 2118.

WAR DIARY
or
INTELLIGENCE SUMMARY.
(Erase heading not required.)

Instructions regarding War Diaries and Intelligence Summaries are contained in F.S. Regs., Part II. and the Staff Manual respectively. Title pages will be prepared in manuscript.

Hour, Date, Place	Summary of Events and Information	Remarks and references to Appendices
22nd June, 1915. LAPUGNOY.	Number of Casualties - Officers 1. Other Ranks 49. Evacuated by No.7 M.A.C. " Nil " 3. Discharged to duty " Nil " 1. Discharged to Convalescent Coy. " Nil " 6.	
23rd June, 1915 LAPUGNOY	No. 237 Cpl T.E. FLAVELL, R.A.M.C. proceeded to 2nd Coldstream Guards for duty. No. 8559 Sgt. H. HALLAMORE, R.A.M.C. and No. 1957 Sgt. MONEY, R.A.M.C. were both wounded at VERMELLES. Number of Casualties - Officers - Nil - Other Ranks 25. Evacuated by No.7 M.A.C. - Nil - " " 7. Discharged to duty - " - 1 " " 2. " Convalescent Coy. Nil - " " 7.	AHG
24th June, 1915. LAPUGNOY and FOUQUIERES.	The following orders received from ADMD 2nd Divn at 5 a.m. 1. No. 4 F.A. will take over the buildings now occupied by No. 3 F.A. at FOUQUIERES by 12 noon today. The Officers Dressing Station at LAPUGNOY will remain open entire other arrangements are made. 2. No 6 F.N. will take over Seminaire St Isaac BETHUNE and buildings at ANNEZIN from No.2 F.A. Ambulance by 9 a.m. today. Completion of moved to be returned to this office. (Signed) O. Sevens Major, for ADMD 2nd Divn.	

Army Form C. 2118.

WAR DIARY
or
INTELLIGENCE SUMMARY.
(Erase heading not required.)

Instructions regarding War Diaries and Intelligence Summaries are contained in F.S. Regs., Part II. and the Staff Manual respectively. Title pages will be prepared in manuscript.

Hour, Date, Place	Summary of Events and Information	Remarks and references to Appendices
24th June, 1915. LABUGNY and FOUQUIERES.	(see C.O.'s note) The Field Ambulance paraded at 10 a.m. and marched off under Capt. O'KEEFFE, R.A.M.C. arriving at FOUQUIERES by 12 noon. The Officer Commanding, the Quarter Master and Adjutant rode to FOUQUIERES and arrived at 11·30 a.m., and took over the Farm but not the Château. The Officers were bivouaced in one field and the men in another. The N.C.O's and new N.S.C. and Workshop Children also bivouaced in field. There was a roomy barn with room for at least 200 beds. In the School there was a dressing room and ward room with accommodation for 20 patients. There were also overflow wards with 20 beds if required, and 2 offices. In the yard of the Château was a Dining Room for patients, Quarter Masters Office, Sleeping place for men on night motor duty &c., and a Carpenter's and Shoemaker's Shop. The Horses were picketted close by the yard where the wagons were parked. The Sergeants mess was in a separate house. Special latrines, grease pits, and incinerators were built for all of those separate compounds.	[signature]

No. 4 Field Ambulance.

Sick and wounded admitted during 24 hours ended 9 am. 22/6/15.

Unit - 2nd Divⁿ	Officers Sick	Officers Wnd.	Other Ranks Sick	Other Ranks Wnd.
2nd Gren. Gds.			2	-
2nd Colds. Gds.			3	-
3rd Colds. Gds.		2	2	-
1st. Irish Gds.			3	1
1st. Herts.	1	-	4	-
1st. Irish Gds.			1	-
2nd H.L.I.			3	1
2nd Horses.			1	-
S. Irish Hse.			1	-
9. H.L.I. 2nd Amm. Tns				15
A.C.C. 2nd Div.			2	-
RAMC 4 F.A.				1
R.F.A. 36 Bde			1	-
R.E. 11th Co.				1
Total.	1	2	23	20

Other Divs.
1st. Queens.			4	-
~~2nd~~				
R.F.A. 6 Lond.			2	
Total	-	-	6	

To Duty
2nd Gren Gds. 1.
Conv. Coy.
2nd H.L.I. 2.
1st. Irish Gds. 2.
1st. Herts. 1.
R.E. 11th Co. 1.
6

Influenza 10.

	Sick	Wnd.
Remain^g Officers	1	2
" other Rks.	29	20
Evac'd Officers		
" other Rks.	3	-
Remng. Officers	5	-
" other Rks.	31	2

Evac'd m A.C.
Officers Nic
Other Rks. 3

To Duty
Officers Nic
Other Rks. 1.
Conv. Coy.
Other Rks. 6.

Trans. No. 5 F.A.
         Wnd. Sick
Officers   2   -
Other Rks. 19 6.

Trans. No 6 F.A.
Officers - -
Other Rks. - 2.

Lieut. T. P. GIBBONS, 1st. Herts.
  G. F. WHIDBORN, 2nd Colds Gds. Shell wnd R. Buttock
2nd Lt. R. P. ELWIS, 3rd Colds. Gds. G.S.W. L. WRIST.

A.D.M.S. 2nd Divⁿ   P. A. Shipp?   Capt. RAMC.
22/6/15.   O.C. No. 4 F.A.

No. 4 Field Ambulance.

Cases transferred to Nos. 5 and 6 Fd. Ambces.
24 hrs ended 9 am. 22/6/15.

No. 5 Field Ambulance.

	Officers		Other Rks.	
	Sick	Wnd.	Sick	Wnd.
A.C.C. 2nd Dvn			2	-
S. Irish Horse			1	-
2nd R. Innis. Fus. Inniskilling			-	15
1st Irish Guards			1	1
9 H.L.I.			-	1
2 H.L.I.			-	1
2 Colds. G.D.			1	-
3 Colds "	-	2	1	-
R.F.A. 6 Lond			1	-
R.E. 11 Coy.			-	1
Total	-	2	6	19

No. 6 Field Ambulance.

1st Irish Guards			1	
2nd Worcesters			1	
Total	-	-	2	-

P.H. Lordmell
Capt. RAMC.
OC. No. 4 Fd. Ambce.

A.D.M.S. 2nd Divn
22/6/15.

No. 4 Field Ambce.
Sick and wounded by units admitted during 24 hrs. ended 9 a.m. 24/6/15.

Unit. 2nd Divⁿ	Officers Sick	Officers Wnd.	Other Rks. Sick	Other Rks. Wnd.	To Duty
2nd Gren Gds.	1	–	1	2	1st Queens 2
2nd Colds "	–	–	7	1	R.F.A 49 Bat. 1 } 5
3rd Colds "	–	–	2	–	2nd Gren Gds. 1
RAMC. 4 F.A.	1	–	–	–	A.S.C. 47 D.T. 1
2nd H.L.I.	–	–	1	–	Conv. Coy.
R.E. 31 Fort. Co.	1	–	–	–	1st Queens 2
2nd Worcs.	–	–	2	–	1st Irish Gds. 1
1st. Irish Gd.	–	–	1	–	1st Herts. 1
2nd R. Innis. Fus.	–	–	–	1	2 H.L.I. 2
S. Irish Horse	–	–	1	–	2 Gren Gds. 1
R.F.A. 39 B.A.C.	–	–	1	–	S.I. Horse 1
					2 Colds. 1
	4	–	16	4	9

Evac^d. M.A.C.
Officers Nil
Other Rks. 5
Duty
Officers Nil
Other Rks. 5
Conv. Coy.
Other Rks. 9

Influenza 4
      Sick Wnd.
Admitted Officers 4 –
 "   Other Rks. 16 4
Evac'd Officers – –
 "   Other Rks. 5 –
Remn^g Officers 8 –
 "   Other Rks. 20 1

Trans^d to 5 Fd. Ambce. Officers Sick 1. Other Rks. Sick 5 Wnd. 4.

Lieut. E.D. POWELL, R.E. 31 Fortress Co.
Capt. C.E. DYAS, RAMC. No.4 F.A. Impetigo
2nd Lt. E.G. WILLIAMS, 2nd Gren. Gds.
Capt. W.L. BRODIE, V.C., 2nd H.L.I. Foll. Tonsillitis.

P.A. Hort Jones
Capt. RAMC.
OC. No.4 F.A.

A.D.M.S. 2nd Divⁿ
24/6/15.

Army Form C. 2118.

WAR DIARY
or
INTELLIGENCE SUMMARY.

(Erase heading not required.)

Hour, Date, Place	Summary of Events and Information	Remarks and references to Appendices
24th June, 1915. LAPUGNOY and FOUQUIERES.	Cars bringing in cases drew up at the School and returned along the road running EAST without coming into the compound. No wagons were allowed to enter the Chateau grounds. The wagons of No. 7 M.A.C. for evacuation were to enter and leave by the gate on West side of Chateau in case of large quantities of casualties. Number of casualties Officers 4 Other Ranks 20. Evacd by No. 7 M.A.C. " Nil " " 5. Discharged to Duty " Nil " " 5. Convalescent Coy. — Nil — 9.	[signature]
25th June, 1915 FOUQUIERES	Capt. E. E. Dyas, R.A.M.C., No. 4 F.A. admitted to Officers' Dressing Station with Impetigo. Number of casualties — Officers 3 Other Ranks 31. Evacd by No. 7 M.A.C. " 1 " " 11. Discharged to Duty " 3 " " 3. Conv. Coy. " 1 " " 7.	

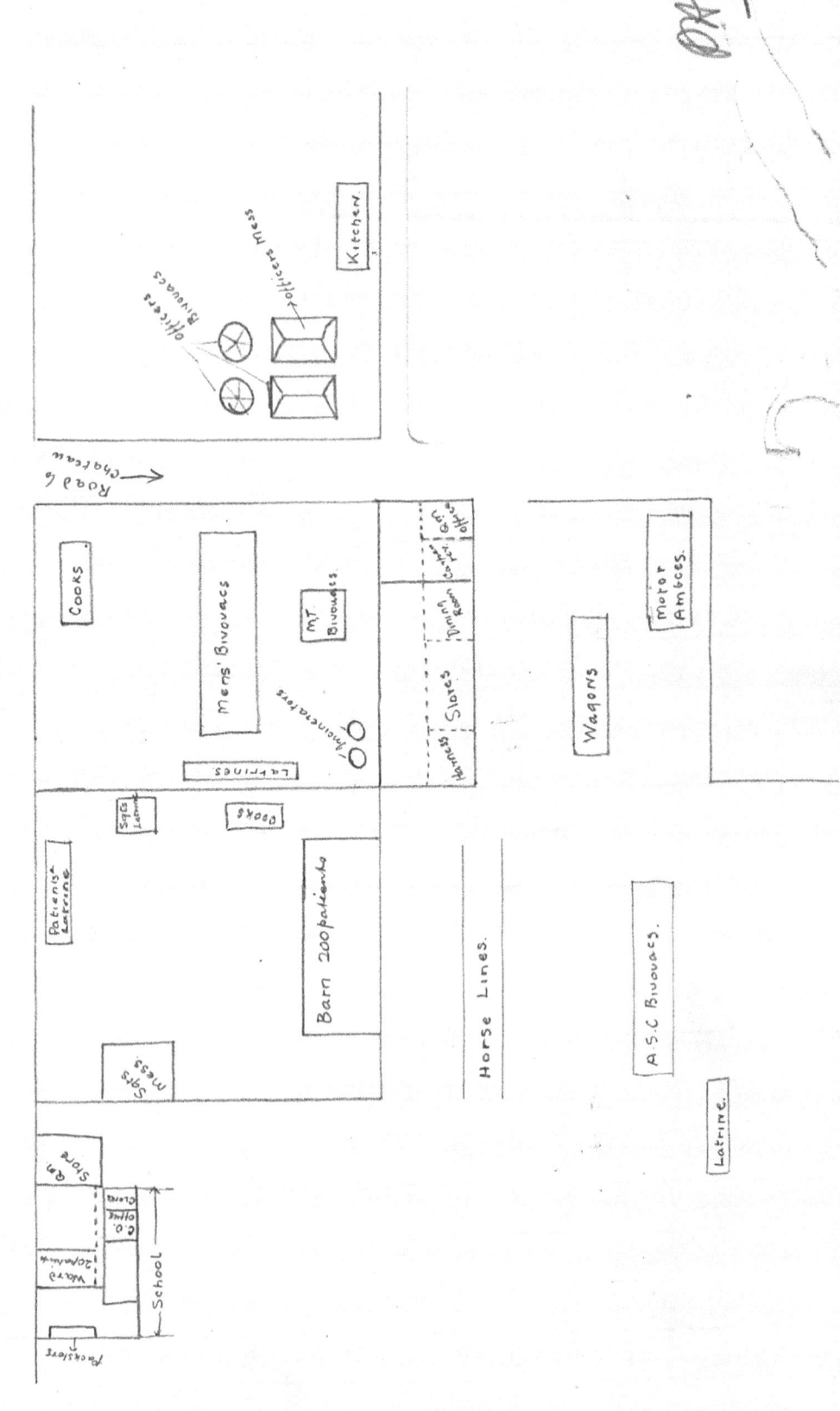

Army Form C. 2118.

WAR DIARY
or
INTELLIGENCE SUMMARY.
(Erase heading not required.)

Instructions regarding War Diaries and Intelligence Summaries are contained in F.S. Regs., Part II. and the Staff Manual respectively. Title pages will be prepared in manuscript.

Hour, Date, Place	Summary of Events and Information	Remarks and references to Appendices
26th June, 1915 FOUQUIERES	Number of Casualties. Officers 1 Other Rks. 20 Evac'd by No 7 M.A.C. " 1 " 4. Discharged to Duty " nil " 2. " Convalescent Coy. " Nil " 9.	
27th June 1915	The Officers' Dressing Station was 1 moved from LAPUGNOY this morning and established in the Chateau PRIEUR St PRY, about 500 yards N.E. of main dressing station. There is accommodation here for 10 Officers, and, if necessary, this could be increased to 20. Lieut B.N. Murphy R.A.M.C. M.O. i/c of Officers Dressing Station. Number of Casualties - Officers Nil Other Ranks 35. Evacuated by No 7 M.A.C. " 1 " 7. Discharges to Duty " Nil " 9. " Convalescent Coy. " Nil " 2.	OHS
28th June, 1915.	The ADVNL 2nd DIVN inspects the Dressing Station this morning The following orders from ADVNL 2nd DIVN was received in the afternoon. No. 4 F.A will move tomorrow morning to VENDIN LES BETHUNE and open there. One section will be opened at OBLINGHEM. (Signed) O'Deuca. Major, for ADVNL 2nd DIVN	

No. 4 Field Ambulance

Sick and wounded admitted 24 hrs ended 9am, 26/6/15

Unit - 2nd Div.	Officers		Other Rks.	
	Sick	Wnd.	Sick	Wnd.
2nd Colds. Gds.			4	1
3rd Colds. Gds.			1	3
1st Irish Gds.			3	-
2nd Oxfords.			2	-
2nd Worcesters.			1	-
R.E. 2nd Sig. Co.			1	-
R.F.A. 48 Batt.			1	-
14 Batt.			1	-
A.S.C. att. 47 Bat. R.F.A.			1	-
R.F.A. 36th Bde.	1			
Total.	1		15	4

To Duty.
Officers -
Other Rks.
2nd Sussex. 1.
2nd Colds. 1.
Conv. Coy.
2nd Oxfds. 1.
2. Tran. SA. 2.
2 Sussex. 2.
1 Irish. 1.
2 Colds. 1.
2 Worces. 1.
3 Colds. 1.
            —
            9

Other Divs.

	Officers		Other Rks.	
	Sick	Wnd.	Sick	Wnd.
2nd Sussex	1	1	1	
Total.	-	-	1	-

Evac'd M.A.C.
Officers 1
Other Rks. 4
To Duty.
Officers
Other Rks. 2
Conv. Coy.
Other Rks. 9
Trans. to No. 5 Fd. Amb. sick 1 wnd 3
Trans. to No. 6 Fd. Amb. sick 3 wnd -

		Sick	Wnd.
Admitted	Officers	1	-
	Other Rks.	16	4
Evac'd	Officers	1	-
	Other Rks.	4	-
Remng.	Officers	7	-
	Other Rks.	23	1

No. 5 Fd. Amb.	Officers		Other Rks.		No. 6 F.A.	Officers		Other Rks.	
	Sick	Wnd	Sick	Wnd		Sick	Wnd	Sick	Wnd
3rd Colds.	-	-	-	3	2nd Colds.	-	-	2	-
A.S.C. (47 Bat R.F.A.)	-	-	1	-	2nd Oxfds.	-	-	1	-
	-	-	1	3		-	-	3	-

Major H.H. HULTON, 36th Bde. R.F.A. Neurasthenia.

A.D.M.S. 2nd Div.
26/6/15.

Capt. R.A.M.C.
O.C. No. 4 F.A.

No. 4 Field Ambulance

Sick and wounded admitted 24 hours ended 9 am 27/6/15.

2nd Div. Unit	Officers Sick	Officers Wnd	Other Rks Sick	Other Rks Wnd
2nd Gren. Gds.			1	–
2nd Colds. Gds.			3	–
3rd Colds. Gds.			1	–
1st Irish Gds.			7	–
1st Herts			1	–
2nd Innis. Fus.			5	1
2nd Worces.			3	1
2nd S. Staffs.			2	–
1st Kings.			1	–
2nd Oxfords.			3	–
2nd K.R.R.			1	–
1st R. Berks			–	1
R.G.A. 111 H. Batt.			1	–
R.F.A. Gr. Batt.			1	–
R.E. 11th Fd. Co.			1	–
9th H.L.I.			–	1
Total	–	–	31	4

To Duty
2 H.L.I. 1
1 Irish Gds. –
2 Worces. 1
2 K.R.R. 1
2 Colds. 1
3 Colds. 1
2 S. Staffs. 1
2 Gren. Gds. 1
— 7 —

Con. Coy.
2 Gren. Gds. 1
2 Colds. 1
— 2 —

Evac. to M.A.C.
Officers – 1
Other Rks. 7

To Duty
Officers nil
Other Rks. 7

Con. Coy
Other Rks. 2

Trans. No. 5 Fd. Amb. 4 sick 2 wnd.

Influenza 4.

	Officers Sick	Officers Wnd	Other Rks Sick	Other Rks Wnd
Admitted officers	–	–	31	4
To duty officers	1	–	7	–
Remaining officers	–	–	32	3

Trans. No 5 Fd. Amb.	Officers S	Officers W	Other Rks S	Other Rks W
2nd Worces.	–	–	1	1
2nd Oxfd.	–	–	1	–
R.F.A. G Batt.	–	–	1	–
1st Irish Gds.	–	–	1	–
1st R. Berks	–	–	–	1
	–	–	4	2

A.D.M.S. 2nd Divn.
27/6/15.

P.A. Lloyd Jones
Capt. RAMC
OC No 4 F.A.

No. 4 Field Ambulance.

Sick and wounded admitted by Units, 24 hours ended 9am. 28/7/15.

Unit. 2nd Dvn	Officers		Other Rks.	
	Sick	Wnd.	Sick	Wnd.
2nd Grem. Gds.			6	-
1st. Irish "			2	1
1st. Herts.			3	1
2nd Oxfords.			3	4
2nd Worcer.			2	1
2nd R. Innis. Ins.			2	1
2nd H.L.I.			1	-
5th. Kings.			1	-
9th. Kings.		2		1
R.G.A. 6 Sge Batt.			1	
M.M.C. Sec. 2 Div			1	-
R.F.A. 48 Batt.			1	-
A.S.C. (M.T.) 4 F.A.			1	
R.A.M.C. 4 F.A.			1	
Total.	2		23	8
Other Dvns				
1st. Leicesters.			1	-
2nd Queens	/1	/1	1	-
R.F.A. 5 Lond.			3	-
Total.	-	-	5	-

Evac'd M.A.C.
Officers - 1
Other Rks. - 4
To Duty
Officers -
Other Rks. 2
Conv. Conv.
Other Rks. 6
Trans. No. 5 Fd. Amb. Sick 1 wnd 2
Trans. No 6 Fd. Amb. Sick 1 wnd. -

To Duty.
R.G.A. 6 S.B. M.B. . 1.
2. R. Innis . 1.
               —
               2.

Conv. Coy.
2. J. Horse . 1.
2. S. Staffs . 1.
R.F.A. Sh.n. . 1.
1 Irish Gds. . 1.
2 Colds. . 1.
2 Worces. . 1.
               —
               6.

No. 5 Fd. Ambul.   S.   W.
2nd Oxfords.   -   2
2nd Grem. Gds.   1   -
                   —   —
                   1   2

No 6. F. A.   S.   W.
2nd Grem. Gds.   1   -

                         Sick wnd.
Admitted Officers 2   -
         Other Rks. 28   8
Evac'd   Officers   1   -
         Other Rks. 3   1
Remng   Officers   7   -
         Other Rks. 45   8

Lieut. S.T.J. PARRY, 9th. Kings.
2nd Lt. T.W.L. PARKER, 9th. Kings.

Influenza.
V.D.H.

[signature]
Capt. R.A.M.C.
O.C. No. 4 F.A.

A.D.M.S. 2nd Dvn
28/6/15.

Army Form C. 2118.

WAR DIARY
or
INTELLIGENCE SUMMARY.
(Erase heading not required.)

Instructions regarding War Diaries and Intelligence Summaries are contained in F.S. Regs., Part II. and the Staff Manual respectively. Title pages will be prepared in manuscript.

Hour, Date, Place	Summary of Events and Information	Remarks and references to Appendices
28th June, 1915. FOUQUIERES -	Number of Casualties - Officers 2 Other Ranks 36. Evac'd by No 7 M.A.C. " 1 " 4 Discharged to Duty " 1 " 2 " . Convalescent Coy. " 1 " 6 (less C Section)	PMO
29th June, 1915 FOUQUIERES - VENDIN-LES-BETHUNE.	Off. under Capt. O'KEEFFE, R.A.M.C. arriving at VENDIN at about 3.30pm. A field on N.W. side of Road in VENDIN was used as an encampment for the troops. Accommodation for 80 patients was made in bell tents and one operating tent. B Section alone is open. The Field Ambulance paraded at 2pm and marched Accommodation for about 40 sick - only serious cases - was found in the schools. The office was temporarily fixed in the schools - later it will be in two separate tents, one of which will be used as the Commanding Officer and the other for the clerks. Billets for Officers, Officers' Mess and Sergeants Mess were arranged in the village. At 5pm the A.D.M.S. 2nd Divn visited & expressed his satisfaction with the arrangements made.	

Army Form C. 2118.

WAR DIARY
or
INTELLIGENCE SUMMARY.
(Erase heading not required.)

Instructions regarding War Diaries and Intelligence Summaries are contained in F. S. Regs., Part II. and the Staff Manual respectively. Title pages will be prepared in manuscript.

Hour, Date, Place	Summary of Events and Information	Remarks and references to Appendices
29th June, 1915. VENDIN-LES-BETHUNE.	Capt. W. McK. H. McCullagh, R.A.M.C. (S.R.) was sent to No.1 Casualty Clearing Station, suffering from N.Y.D. fever. Number of casualties - Officers 1, other Ranks 17. Evacuated by No.7 M.A.C. " 3 - " 22. Discharged to duty " 4 - " 11. " Convalescent Coy. " Nil - " 21. The attached is a rough plan of the encampment at VENDIN.	PK9.

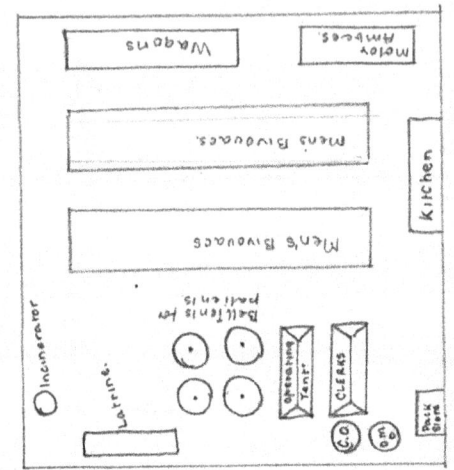

No. 4 Field Ambulance.

Sick and wounded, by Units, admitted during 24 hours ended 9am. 29/6/15.

2nd Div. Unit.	Officers		Other Rks.	
	Sick	Wnd.	Sick	Wnd.
2nd Oxfords.			1	4
2nd Worcs.			3	1
2nd H.L.I.			6	–
R.F.A. H.Q.			1	–
41 B.A.C.			1	–
R.E. 2 Sig Co.	1	–	–	–
Total.	1	–	12	5

Evac. M.A.C.
Officers. 3
Other Rks. 22
To Duty
Officers 4
Other Rks. 11
Conv. Coy.
Other Rks. 21

	Sick	Wnd.
Admitted Officers	1	–
Other Rks.	12	5
Evac'd Officers	3	–
Other Rks.	20	2
Remaining Officers	1	–
Other Rks.	4	2

Transferred to 5 F.A.   Sick Wnd.
	Sick	Wnd.
2nd Worcs.	3	1
2nd Oxfords.	1	4
Total.	4	5

Trans. No. 6 F.A.   1   –
                    1   –

Lieut. B. HOWARTH, R.E. 2nd Sig Co,   Influenza.

P.H. Lloyd Jones.
Capt. R.A.M.C.
O.C. No. 4 Fd. Am.

A.D.M.S. 2nd Div'n
29/6/15.

Army Form C. 2118.

WAR DIARY
or
INTELLIGENCE SUMMARY.
(Erase heading not required.)

Hour, Date, Place	Summary of Events and Information	Remarks and references to Appendices
30th June. 1915. VENDIN-LES-BETHUNE.	No 3684 Pte MADGE, J. R.A.M.C. No.4 F.A. was evacuated by No.7 M.A.C. with Appendicitis. The Aire Road was used on 4 Officers, -2 2nd Grenadiers, 2 2nd Coldstream Guards, - for Commissions in the Regular Forces. All the Officers were found fit. Number of casualties. Officers 1. Other Ranks 2. Evacuated by No.7 M.A.C. " 1 - Nil.	PMQ

No. 4 Field Ambulance.

Sick and wounded admitted, by Units, during 24 hours ended 9am. 30/6/15.

Unit: 2nd Divn	Officers Sick	Officers Wnd	Other Rks Sick	Other Rks Wnd	Remarks.
1st Irish Guards	—	—	1	—	Trans. No. 5 F.H.
RAMC 4 F.A.	1	—	—	—	
15th Hrs. (H.Q.2D)	—	—	1	—	— do —
	1	—	2	—	

Cmg'd M.A.C.
    Nil
To Duty Officers.
    Nil
Convr Coy
    Nil
Trans. No. 5 F.A.
    2 sick. (see above).

                         Sick   Wnd
Admitted Officers   1   —
        "   Other Rks   2   —
Evacuated Officers   1   —
        "   Other Rks   —   —
Remng. Officers   1   —
        "   Other Rks   4   2.

Capt. W. Mc.K. H. McCULLAGH, RAMC. No.4 F.A.
                 N.Y.D. Fever.

                         P.A. Lloyd Jones
                         Capt. RAMC
                         O.C. No. 4 Fd. Amb.

A.D.M.S. 2nd Divn
     30/6/15.

121/6306

121/6306 2nd 2-/5 Division

No 4. Field Ambulance

Vol ~~XXI~~ XII

To Gen De la Rey

July '15

Army Form C. 2118

WAR DIARY
or
INTELLIGENCE SUMMARY
(Erase heading not required.)

Place	Date	Hour	Summary of Events and Information	Remarks and references to Appendices
VENDIN	1/7/15		Number of Casualties:- 8 sick 1 wnd.D. Officers Nil. Evacuated by No 7 M.A.C. 1 sick. Discharged to duty Nil. Convalescent Coy. 3.	
"	2/7/15		Capt. G. B. Dyas, R.A.M.C. returned to duty. Lieut. A.G.H. Lowe posted to 1st R. Berks Regt for temporary duty. Number of Casualties 1 sick. Evacuated by No. 7 M.A.C. 1 sick. Discharged to duty Nil. Convalescent Coy. 2.	
"	3/7/15		Lieut H.M. Cockcroft R.A.M.C. to temporary duty with 2nd S. Staffs. Number of Casualties:- Nil.	
"	4/7/15		No. 8194 Pte Christian G, R.A.M.C. evacuated to Base with Nephritis. No. 6218 S/Sgt Cockerill R.W. R.A.M.C. proceed to England on 7 days leave. Number of Casualties- Officers Nil. Other Ranks 1 sick. Evacuated by 7 M.A.C. 1 sick. Discharged to duty - Nil. Convalescent Coy - 1.	

Army Form C. 2118

WAR DIARY
or
INTELLIGENCE SUMMARY

(Erase heading not required.)

Instructions regarding War Diaries and Intelligence Summaries are contained in F.S. Regs., Part II. and the Staff Manual respectively. Title Pages will be prepared in manuscript.

Place	Date	Hour	Summary of Events and Information	Remarks and references to Appendices
VENDIN	5/7/15		No. 5 Field Ambulance are at Ecole Maternelle, Bethune and a bearer Sub-Division near Cauchy. No. 6 Field Ambulance at College St. Vaast Bethune. Both 2o Ambces are open. No. 18119 Pte Boyre, J. evacuated to Base with Bronchitis. Lieut R. H. E. Henley, 2nd Coldstream Guards admitted suffering with diarrhoea, and was treated in Officers' Billets. Lieut Oudain. French Interpreter was admitted and transferred to CHOQUES to No. 1 Casualty Clearing Station. Number of Casualties. Officers 1. Other Ranks 3. Evacuated by No. 7 M.A.C. Officers 1 " " 4. Discharged to duty Nil. - Convalescent Coy. Nil.	CHQ
"	6/7/15		A.D.M.S. 2nd Divn. inspected the Field Ambulance accompanied by A/Capt. 37th Divn. Lieut HM- Cockeroft R.A.M.C. returned from temporary duty with 2nd S Staffs Regt. Number of Casualties Officers 1. Other Ranks 1. Evacuated by No. 7 M.A.C. 1 Sick. Discharged to duty Nil. - Convalescens Company 2.	

No 4 Field Ambulance

Sick & wounded admitted, by Unit, during 24 hours ended 9 a.m. 6/7/15.

2nd Div Units	Officers		Other ranks	
	Sick	Wnd	Sick	Wnd
2nd Cold. Gds	1	–	1	–
	1	–	1	–

	Sick	Wnd
Admitted Officers	1	–
" Other rks	1	–
Evacd. Officers	–	–
" Other rks	1	–
Remaining Officers	1	–
" Other rks	7	1

Evacd M.A.C.
  Officers nil
  Other rks 1
To Duty nil
Con. Coy.
  Sick 1   2nd Gren. Gds
  Wnd 1 2   —do—

Evacuated Sick
RAMC No 4 Fd Amb 1

Officer admitted
2nd Cold. Guards. Lieut A.H.E. ASHLEY Diarrhoea

P.A. [signature]
Capt. RAMC
O.C. No 4 Field Amb.

ADMS 2nd Div.
6/7/15

No 4 Field Ambulance

Sick & wounded admitted, by Units, during 24 hours ended 9 am. 7/7/15.

2nd Div Units	Officers Sick	Officers wnd	Other Rks Sick	Other Rks wnd		
R.F.A. 2nd D.A.C.	—	—	1	—	To Corr. Coy.	
7th Kings	—	—	1	—	2nd Green Gds.	1
					2nd Cold. Gds.	2
						3
	—	—	2	—		

Evacd. M.A.C.
  Officers   nil
  Other rks. 2
To Duty   nil
Corr. Coy.
  sick 3
  wnd nil 3

	Sick	Wnd
Admitted Officers	—	—
" Other rks	2	—
Evacd Officers	—	—
" Other ranks	2	—
Remaining Officers	1	—
" Other rks	4	1

Evacuated Sick
  A.S.C. No 2 Co. 1
  R.F.A. 2nd D.A.C. 1
                          2

A.D.M.S. 2nd Div.
7/7/15

P.A Lloyd Jones
Capt RAMC
O.C. No 4 Field Amb.

Army Form C. 2118

WAR DIARY
or
INTELLIGENCE SUMMARY
(Erase heading not required.)

Instructions regarding War Diaries and Intelligence Summaries are contained in F.S. Regs., Part II. and the Staff Manual respectively. Title Pages will be prepared in manuscript.

Place	Date	Hour	Summary of Events and Information	Remarks and references to Appendices
VENDIN	7/7/15		Lieut B.N. Murphy, R.A.M.C. proceeded to 1st R. Berks Regt. for temporary duty vice Lieut Lowe, R.A.M.C. proceeding to Boulogne for duty. One Bearer Sub. Division was ordered by A.D.M.S. 2nd Divn. to aid in lining the streets near Bethune on the occasion of the visit of Lord Kitchener to the troops in the area. Number of Casualties — Officers Nil Other Ranks 2 sick. Evacuated by No. 7 M.A.C. Officers Nil " " 2 " Discharged to Duty - Nil. " " Convalescent Coy. 3.	A.D.S.
"	8/7/15		Lieut A.R. Moorhouse, R.A.M.C. arrived for duty from No. 25 Fd. Amble. Number of Casualties officers. Nil Other Ranks 3. Evacuated by No. 7 M.A.C. 1 sick.	
"	9/7/15		Lieut A.H.A. Morton R.A.M.C. proceeded for temporary duty with 2nd R. Inniskilling Fusiliers. Number of Casualties - officers nil other Ros nil. Evacuated by No. 7 MAC 1 officer sick. Discharged to Duty 1.	
"	10/7/15		Number of Casualties Nil. Discharged to Convalescent Coy 1.	

No. 4 Field Ambulance

Sick & wounded admitted, by Units, during 24 hours ended 9 a.m. 8/7/15.

2nd Div. Units	Officers		Other ranks	
	Sick	Wnd.	Sick	Wnd.
1st R. Berks	—	—	2	1
	—	—	2	1

Evacd. M.A.C.   admitted   Officers   Sick Wnd
  Officers   nil   "   Other rks   2   1
  Other rks   1   evacuated   Officers   —   —
To Duty   nil   "   Other rks   1   —
Con. Coy   nil   Remaining   Officers   1   —
                                                                                                               "   Other rks   5   2

Evacuated sick
2nd Oxf & Bucks   1

P. A. Lloyd Jones.

A.D.M.S. 2nd Div.
8/7/15

Capt Rame
O.C. No 4 Fd Amb

No 4 Field Ambulance

Sick & wounded admitted, by units,
during 24 hours ended 9 a.m. 9/7/15

2nd Div. Units	Officers		Other ranks	
	Sick	Wnd	Sick	Wnd
	nil			

To Duty:-
   1st Berks   1

				Sick	Wnd
Evacd. M.A.C.		Admitted Officers		–	–
Officers	1	" Other rks		–	–
Other ranks	nil	Evacuated Officers		1	–
To Duty		" Other rks		–	–
Other ranks (Wounded)	1	Remaining Officers		–	–
Con. Coy	nil	" Other rks		5	1

Evacuated Sick (Officer)
{ 2nd Coldstream Guards 1.
  1 Lieut. A.H.E. ASHLEY (Diarrhoea)

ADMS 2nd Division
9/7/15

P.H. Lloyd Jones
Capt. R.A.M.C.
O/C No 4 Fd Ambce

No 4 Field Ambulance

Sick & wounded admitted, by units,
during 24 hours ended 10/7/15.

	Officers		Other rks	
	Sick	Wnd	Sick	Wnd
	nil			

To Con. boy:-
7th Kings   1

                                                   Sick Wnd

Evac^d M.A.C.   Admitted Officers — nil —
   Officers   nil   " Other rks — nil —
   Other rks nil   Evac^d Officers — nil —
To Duty   nil   " Other rks — nil —
Con. Coy II Div: Remaining Officers — nil —
   Other rks (sick) 1   " Other rks 4 1

P. H. Lloyd Jones.

A.D.M.S. 2nd Div.   Capt. R.A.M.C.
10/7/15   O.C. No 4 Field Amb.

No 4 Field Ambce.

Sick & wounded admitted, by Units, during 24 hours ended 11/7/15.

	Officers		Other ranks	
	sick	wnd	sick	wnd
To 2nd Div. Con. Coy				
1st Berks			1	

Nil

				sick	wnd
Evacd. M.A.C.		Admitted Officers		— nil —	
Officers	nil	" Other rks		— nil —	
Other rks	"	Evacd Officers		— nil —	
To Duty	nil	" Other rks		— nil —	
To 2nd Div. Con. Coy		Remaining Officers		— nil —	
Other ranks (sick)	1	" Other rks		3	1

P.R. Lloyd Jones

ADMS
2nd Div.
11/7/15

Capt. R.A.M.C.
O.C. No 4 Field Amb

Army Form C. 2118

WAR DIARY
or
INTELLIGENCE SUMMARY
(Erase heading not required.)

Instructions regarding War Diaries and Intelligence Summaries are contained in F. S. Regs., Part II and the Staff Manual respectively. Title Pages will be prepared in manuscript.

Place	Date	Hour	Summary of Events and Information	Remarks and references to Appendices
VENDIN	10/7/15		Capt. J.J. O'Keeffe. R.A.M.C. and Lieut. A.J. Andrews. R.A.M.C. returned from leave. Capt. D. Maclellan, R.A.M.C. (S.R.) arrived for temporary duty from No.1. Casualty Clearing Station, vice Capt. G.E. Byas, R.A.M.C. who proceeded to No.1 C.C.S. for temporary duty. April 1st Corps visited the Dressing Station. Lieut. E.R.B. Smyth, 7th Kings Regt. admitted with contusion R. Leg & was evacuated by No.7 M.A.C. same evening. 1 N.C.O. and 8 men were temporarily attached to H.Q. and own Signals for instruction in telephone work. Commanding Officer, Capt. O'Keeffe, S/Sgts. Pepper and Moor went to a demonstration on the use of Smoke Helmets which was held at 6th Infty. Bde. H.Q.	PRS.
"	12/7/15		Capt. Large, R.A.M.C. joined for duty from 1st. R. Berks. The following orders were received by from Hd.qrd. 2nd Divn. 1. No.4 Field Ambce. will move to Bethune forthwith and take over the Ecole Maternelle and the evacuation of the Curchy section from No.6 Fd. Ambce. 2. No.5 Fd. Amb. will move to Vendin and take over the buildings at present occupied by No.4 Fd. Ambce.	

(Signed) O. Severs. Major. R.A.M.C.
         Comdg. 2nd Divn.

No 4 Field Ambulance

Sick & wounded admitted by Unit, during 24 hours ended 9 a.m. 12/7/15

2 Div Unit.	Officers		Other ranks	
	Sick	wnd	Sick	wnd.
7th Kings	1	—	—	—
	1	—	—	—

				sick	wnd
Evacⁿ M.A.C.		Admitted Officers		1	nil
Officers	1	" Other ranks		nil	nil
Other rks	nil	Evac^d Officers		1	nil
To Duty	nil	" Other rks		nil	nil
To 2nd Div. Con Coy	nil	Remaining Officers		nil	nil
		" Other rks		3	1

Officer Admitted Sick

7th Kings 2nd Lt. G.R.G. SMYTH Contusion Rt Leg (Horse Kick)

Officer Evacuated Sick

7th Kings 1 (2nd Lt. G.R.G. SMYTH)

R.H. Lloyd Jones
Capt R.A.M.C.
O.C. No 4 Field Amb.

A.D.M.S 2nd Division
12/7/15

No 4 Field Ambulance

Sick & wnd. admitted, by units, during 24 hours ended 9 a.m. 13/7/15.

	Officers		Other ranks	
	Sick	Wnd	Sick	Wnd
			nil	

Evac^d M.A.C   nil   Admitted   sick   wnd

To Duty   nil   Officers — nil —

To 2nd Div. Con Coy. nil   Other rks — nil —

                               Evac^d

                               Officers — nil —

                               Other rks — nil —

                               Remaining

                               Officers — nil —

                               Other rks   3   1

P.H. Lloyd Jones

ADMS 2nd Division   Capt RAMC
13/7/15   o/c No 4 Field Amb.

WAR DIARY
or
INTELLIGENCE SUMMARY
(Erase heading not required.)

Army Form C. 2118

Instructions regarding War Diaries and Intelligence Summaries are contained in F.S. Regs., Part II. and the Staff Manual respectively. Title Pages will be prepared in manuscript.

Place	Date	Hour	Summary of Events and Information	Remarks and references to Appendices
VENDIN (Continued)	12/7/15		The following orders was received from H.Q.H.S. 2nd Div. The move ordered in my M.B 587 will take place early tomorrow morning. (Signed) O. Severs Major R.A.M.C. for Actind 2nd Div.	
VENDIN to BETHUNE	13/7/15		All the personnel moved from VENDIN to Ecole Maternelle, Bethune, with the exception of Bearer Sub-Division of "C" Section & Cooks, &c, to No. 1 Harley Street. One N.C.O. and 2 men were sent to take over the Schools at BEUVRY.	OK4
BETHUNE	14/7/15		Commanding officer proceeded to England. Capt. J.J. O'Keefe, R.A.M.C., took over the duties of C.O. The D.D.M.S. 1st. Corps visited the Dressing Station Capt. J.J. O'Keefe, R.A.M.C. visited the Advanced Dressing Stations at BEUVRY and No. 1 Harley Street. The following order was received from H.Q.H.S. 2nd Div. "The Advanced Dressing Stations must have a personnel of 3 Officers of whom one must always be at No. 1 Harley Street and one always at BEUVRY. This allows of reliefs among themselves. (Signed) O. Severs Major for Actind. 2nd Div. Lieut. P.G. WOODHOUSE R.A.M.C. was detailed for duty with O.C. Bearer Sub-Division.	

No. 4 Field Ambulance.

Sick and Wounded admitted by Units during 24 hours ended 9am. 14/7/15.

Units 2nd Divn	Officers Sick	Officers Wnd	Other Rks Sick	Other Rks Wnd	
2nd Gren. Gds.			3	2	
2nd Colds. Gds.			5	2	
3rd Colds. Gds.			2	1	
1st Herts.			1		
1st Queens			1		
2nd Innis Fus.			3		
2nd S. Staffs			1		
5th Kings			2		
R.E. 170 Coy	1	-	-	1	Officer admitted & evac'd.
R.G.A. 15 Bde.			1		2nd Lt. H.H. Yuill, R.E. 170 Co. Dermatitis.
R.F.A. 17 Batt.			1		
" 2. D.A.C.			2		
" 56 Batt			1		
" 30 Batt.			2		
R.G.A. 6 "			1		
R.E. 11th Coy.			1		
7th Kings			1		
	1	-	28	6	

Transferred from No. 5 Fd. Amb.

1st Herts.			1	1	
1st R. Berks					
5th Kings			3		
R.A.M.C. (att 34 B. R.F.A)			1		
R.F.A. 41 Bde.			2		
" 44			1	1	
R.E. 170 Coy			3		
" East Ang.			-	1	
	-	-	11	3	

Evac'd M.AC.   Influenza 7.
Officers One (1)   Admitted Officers   1 - 0
Other Rks 2.   Other Rks. 28 - 6
Duty Nil   Evac'd Officers   1
Conv. Coy Nil   Other Rks. 1 - 1
                                Remaining Officers -
                                          Other Rks. 41 - 9

A.D.M.S. 2nd Divn
14/7/15.

J.J. O'Keeffe
Capt. R.A.M.C.
O.C. No. 4 F.A.

No 4 Field Ambulance
Sick & wounded admitted, by Units,
during 24 hours ended 9 a.m. 15/7/15

2nd Div Units	Officers		Other ranks			
	Sick	Wnd	Sick	Wnd		
2nd Green Gds.	–	–	1	–	To Duty:-	
2nd Cold. Gds	–	–	1	–	Ramc. att 39 Bde	1
3rd Cold. Gds	–	–	4	–	1st Berks	2
1st Irish Gds	–	–	1	1	7th Kings	2
						5
1st Herts	–	–	2	–	To Con. Coy	
2nd Oxf & Bucks	–	–	2	–	2nd Cold. Gds	1
2nd Innis F	–	–	5	–	1st Herts	1
7th Kings	–	–	3	–		2
1st Queens	–	–	2	–		
2nd H.L.I	–	–	3	–		
	–	–	23	1		

Evac. M.A.C.
   Officers nil
   Other ranks 8

Evac. Barge
   Other ranks 1

To Duty
   Other rks (sick) 5

To Con. Coy 2nd Div.
   Other rks sick 1 wnd 2

A.D.M.S 2nd Div.
15/7/15

		Sick	Wnd
Admitted	Officers	0	0
"	Other rks	23	1
Evac	Officers	0	0
"	Other rks	4	5
Remaining	Officers	0	0
"	Other rks	54	4

J. J. O'Keeffe
Capt Ramc
for O.C. No 4 Field Amb.

Army Form C. 2118

WAR DIARY
or
INTELLIGENCE SUMMARY
(Erase heading not required.)

Place	Date	Hour	Summary of Events and Information	Remarks and references to Appendices
BETHUNE	14/7/15		Number of Casualties - Officers 1 Other Ranks 34. Evacuated by No.7 M.A.C. " 1 " " 2	
"	15/7/15		Capt. W. McK H. McCullagh, R.A.M.C. (S.R.) returned from Hospital, Base, for duty. R.A.M.C. 2nd I/c inspected the Dressing Station. Number of Casualties - Officers Nil Other Ranks 24. Evacuated by No.7 M.A.C. " Nil " " 8. " Ambulance Barge " Nil " " 1. Discharged to duty Other Ranks 6. " Convalescent Coy. 2.	PKg
"	16/7/15		Number of Casualties - Officers 1. Other Ranks 27. Evacuated by No.7 M.A.C. " 1 " " 9. Discharged to duty 4 " Convalescent Coy. 4.	
"	17/7/15		No.12656 Sgt McKEOWN, R.A.M.C. proceeded on leave to England for 7 days. Number of Casualties - Officers 5 Other Ranks 37. Evacuated by No.7 M.A.C. " 4 " " 38 Discharged to duty 2 " Convalescent Coy. 3.	

No 4 Field Ambulance
Sick & wounded admitted, by Units,
during 24 hours ended 9 am 16/7/15

Unit	Officers Sick	Officers Wnd	Other ranks Sick	Other ranks Wnd
2nd Grenr Gds	-	-	2	-
3rd Cold. Gds	-	-	5	-
1st Irish Gds	-	-	1	1
1st Werk	-	-	3	-
2nd Oxf & Bucks	-	-	2	-
1st Innis Fusil.	-	-	2	-
3rd BlackW. att.)	1	-	-	-
2nd H.L.I. }				
2nd H.L.I.	-	-	3	-
7th Kings	-	-	1	1
1st Mullins	-	-	1	-
R.F.A. 170th Bratt.	-	-	1	-
" 56th "	-	-	1	-
" 70th "	-	-	1	-
	1	-	22	2

To Duty:
3rd Cold. Gds   1
2nd Inners Fus. 1
2nd H.L.I.   1
                 —
                 3

To 2nd Divn Con. Coy:
2nd Cold. Gds   1
2nd Gren Gds   1
2nd H.L.I.   1
R.F.A. 6th Batt 1
                 —
                 4

Other Divns

Unit	Officers Sick	Officers Wnd	Other ranks Sick	Other ranks Wnd
R.E. 170th Co.	-	-	-	1
R.G.A. 26th H.B	-	-	1	-
R.F.A. 46th Batt.	-	-	1	-
	-	-	2	1

Officer Admitted
3rd BlackW.) 2nd Lt R.A. DOUGLAS
(att: 2nd H.L.I)   Asthma

Influenza: 5

	Sick	Wnd
Evacd By No 7 M.A.C.		
Officers	1	-
Other ranks	8	1
To Duty		
Other ranks	3	-
To Con. Coy 2nd Div.		
Other ranks	4	-
Trans: to No 6 F.Amb		
Other ranks	1	

	Sick	Wnd
Admitted		
Officers	1	-
Other ranks	24	3
Evacd		
Officers	1	-
Other ranks	8	1
Remaining		
Officers	-	-
Other ranks	62	6

J.J. O'Keiffe
Capt. R.A.M.C.
for O.C. No 4 Field Amb:

A.D.M.S. 2nd Div
16th July 1915

No 4 Field Ambulance
Sick & Wounded admitted, by Units,
during 24 hours ended 9 am 17/7/15

2nd Div Units	Officers		Other ranks				
	Sick	Wound	Sick	Wnd.			
2nd Gren Gds	-	-	1	9	To Duty:-		
3rd Cold. Gds	-	-	1	2	1st Queens	1	
1st Irish Gds	1	-	2	-	1st Herts	1	
1st Herts	2	-	1	-		2	
5th Kings	-	-	1	1	To Con. Coy 2nd Div		
17th Kings	-	-	2	-		Sick	Wnd
2nd Innis Fusil	-	-	2	-	3rd Cold. Gds	1	-
1st Oxf Bucks	-	-	2	-	R.F.A. 41st Bde	1	-
2nd H.L.I.	-	-	4	-	1st Queens	1	-
9th H.L.I.	-	-	1	-		3	-
1st Queens	-	-	1	-			
South Irish Horse	1	-	-	-			
R.F.A. 36th Bde A.C.	-	1	-	-			
" 17th Batt.	-	-	1	-			
" 2nd D.A.C.	-	-	-	-			
R.G.A. "	-	-	1	-			
	4	1	20	12			

Other Divns

1st E.R.R. att 130th R.S.	-	-	2	-	
R.G.A. 9th Sege Batt	-	-	1	-	
R.F.A. 3rd D.A.C.	-	-	1	1	Cases Remng 10.
4th R.W.F.	-	-	-	1	
	-	-	4	1	

Evacd By M.A.C.	Sick	Wnd		Admitted	Officers	Sick	Wnd
Officers	3	1				4	1
Other Rks	30	8			Other Rks	24	13
To Duty				Evacd	Officers	3	1
Other Rks	2	0			Other Rks	30	8
To 2nd Div Con. Coy.							
Other returns	3	0		Remaining	Officers	1	0
					Other Rks		

Officers Admitted

1st Herts	2nd Lt K.K. FYFFE	Pleurisy
-do-	Lieut G.M. BROWN	Diarrhoea
1st Irish Gd	2nd Lt R.T.P RODAKOWSKI	Impetigo
R.F.A. 9th B.A.C	Lieut T.R. CLELAND	Wound concussion
S.Irish Horse	2nd Lt C.T. STEWART	Chronic Orychia

A.D.M.S. 2nd Div.
17/7/15

J.J. O'Keeffe
Capt. RAMC
for O.C. No 4 Field Amb

No 4 Field Ambulance
Sick & Wounded admitted, by units,
during 24 hours ended 9 a.m. 15/7/15

2nd Div. Units	Officers		Other ranks				
	Sick	Wnd	Sick	Wnd	To Duty	Sick	Wnd
2nd Cold. Guards	1	-	2	4			
1st Irish Guards	-	-	1	1	1st Queens	1	-
1st Herts	-	-	4	1	R.F.A. 17th Batt	1	-
2nd H.L.I.	-	-	3	-	" 2nd D.A.C	1	-
2nd Oxf & Bucks	-	-	3	-		3	-
2nd Innis Fusil	-	-	3	-			
5th Kings	1	-	1	-			
7th Kings	-	-	1	-	To Con. Coy 2nd Div.		
1st Berks	-	-	2	-	2nd Innis	2	-
9th H.L.I.	-	-	1	-	R.F.A. 2nd DAC	1	-
RAMC att 2nd Innis	-	-	1	-	" 13th Batt	1	-
ASC MT att No 4 F.A	-	-	1	-	R.G.A. 6th Siege	1	-
No 1 M.M.G.S.	-	1	-	-	2nd H.L.I	1	-
	2	1	22	5	2nd O+B	2	-
Other Divns					5th Kings	1	-
R.G.A. 5th Siege	-	-	1	-	1st Herts	1	-
A.S.C. M.T. att R.G.A. (19th Siege B)	-	-	1	1		10	-
R.E.173rd Mining Co	-	-	1	-			
	-	-	2	1	Influenza 5.		

	Sick	Wnd
Admitted Officers	2	1
" Other Rks	24	6
Evac. Officers	3	1
" Other Rks	3	3
Remaining Officers	-	-
" Other Rks	58	13

Evac. by No 7 M.A.C.

	Sick	Wnd
Officers	3	1
Other Rks	3	3

To Duty: Other Rks   3   -
To 2nd Div. Con. Coy
  Other Rks   10   -
Trans. to No 6 Fd Amb.   1   -

Admitted Officers

No 1 M.M.G.S.   Major R.J. COLSON   Wound concussion
2nd Cold. Gds   "   P.A. McGREGOR, D.S.O.   Influenza
5th Kings   2nd Lt. E.S. FORSTER   Influenza

A.D.M.S. 2nd Div.   J.J. O'Keeffe
8/7/15   Capt RAMC
                      O.C. No 4 Field Ambce

Army Form C. 2118

WAR DIARY
or
INTELLIGENCE SUMMARY
(Erase heading not required.)

Instructions regarding War Diaries and Intelligence Summaries are contained in F.S. Regs., Part II. and the Staff Manual respectively. Title Pages will be prepared in manuscript.

Place	Date	Hour	Summary of Events and Information	Remarks and references to Appendices
BETHUNE	18/7/15		Capt. W. McK. H. McCULLAGH, R.A.M.C. (S.R.) proceeded on leave to England for 7 days. No. 38600 Pte Griffiths W.H. and No. 39515 Pte Hilliard, A.J. arrived for duty from 3/5th Highland Field Ambulance. D.A.D.M.S. 2nd Divn. inspected the Dressing Station. Number of Casualties Officers – 3 Other Ranks 30 Evacuated by No 7 M.A.C. " 4 " " 6 Discharged to Duty 3 " Convalescent Coy. 10.	PMS
"	19/7/15		Casualties – Officers Nil Other Ranks 16. Evacuated by No 7 M.A.C. Officers Nil Other Ranks 13. Discharged to Duty 3. " Convalescent Coy. 4.	
"	20/7/15		Number of Casualties- Officers 2 Other Ranks 19. Discharged to Duty " Nil " " 3. " Convalescent Coy " Nil " " 4. Evacuated by No 7 M.A.C. " 1. " " 10	

1875 Wt. W593/826 1,000,000 4/15 J.B.C. & A. A.D.S.S./Forms/C. 2118.

No. 4 Field Ambulance
Sick & wounded admitted, by Units,
during 24 hours ended 19th July, 1915.

2nd Div. Units	Officers		Others	
	Sick	Wnd	Sick	Wnd
2nd Grew Gds.	-	-	1	-
3rd Cold. Gds	-	-	1	1
1st Irish Gds	-	-	1	1
2nd Innis Fusil.	-	-	3	-
2nd H.L.I.	-	-	1	-
2nd O&B	-	-	3	-
A.C.C. 2nd Div.	-	-	1	-
R.F.A. 41st Bde A.C.	-	-	1	-
	1	-	11	1
Other Divns.				
2nd Wilts att 174th R.E.	-	-	1	-
R.F.C.	-	-	1	-
R.G.A. 6th Batt	-	-	1	-
" 26th H.B.	-	-	1	-
			4	-

To Duty:
	Sick	Wnd
2nd Grew Gds	2	-
5th Kings	1	-
	3	-

To 2nd Div. Con. Coy
7th Kings	1	-
R.E. East Ang.	-	1
2nd Oxf & Bucks	-	1
2nd Innis Fus.	1	-
	2	2

Influenza 7.

Evac M.A.C. Sick Wnd
Officers   -   -
Other ranks 11 2

To Duty
Other ranks 3 -
To 2nd Div. Con. Co.
Other ranks 2 2

Admitted Officers Sick Wnd
  -   -
Other Rks 15 1

Evac Officers - -
" Other Rks 11 2

Remaining Officers - -
Other Rks 57 10

J.J. O'Keeffe
Capt. R.A.M.C.
O/C No. 4 Field Amb.

A.D.M.S. 2nd Div.
19/7/15

No 4 Field Ambulance
Sick & wounded admitted, by Unit,
during 24 hours ended 9 a.m. 20/7/15

2nd Div. Unit	Officers		Other Ranks				
	Sick	Wnd	Sick	Wnd	To Duty:	Sick	Wnd
2nd Cold. Guards	-	1	1	-	1st Irish Gds	1	-
3rd "	-	-	2	-	3rd Cold. "	1	-
1st Irish "	-	-	1	-	1st Herts	1	-
2nd Oxf & Bucks	-	-	3	-	To 2nd Div. Con. Coy	3	-
2nd Innis Fusil	1	-	-	-			
2nd South Staffs	-	-	-	-	2nd Green Gds	-	1
2nd H.L.I.	-	-	4	-	2nd Innis Fus	1	-
7th H.L.I.	-	-	1	-	2nd H.L.I.	1	-
2nd Worcesters	-	-	1	-	R.G.A. 26th H.B.	1	-
R.G.A. 44th Bde	-	-	1	-		3	1
R.E. 11th Co	-	-	1	-			
	1	1	16	-			
Other Divisions							
2nd Munsters	-	-	1	1			
R.G.A. 9th Siege B	-	-	1	-			
R.E. 176th Co.	-	-	-	-			
	-	-	2	1			

Evac'd By M.A.C.   Sick Wnd
  Officers   -   -
  Other Ranks   7   3

To Duty
  Other ranks   3   -
To 2nd Div. Con. Coy
  Other ranks   3   1

Admitted   Sick Wnd.
  Officers   1   1
  Other Ranks   18   1

Evacuated
  Officers   1   -
  Other Ranks   7   3

Remaining
  Officers   -   1
  Other Ranks   62   7

Officers Admitted
  2nd S.Staffs. 2nd Lt. C. DUTTON   Syphilis
  2nd Cold.Gds.   "   O.W.H. LEESE   G.S.W. shoulder + face

ADMS 2nd Divn   J.O.Keyff   Capt R.A.M.C.
20/7/15   O.C. No 4 F. Amb.

No 4 Field Ambulance
Sick & wounded admitted, by Unit,
during 24 hours ended 9 am 21/7/15

Unit	Officers Sick	Officers Wnd	Other ranks Sick	Other ranks Wnd
2nd Green Gds	-	1	1	1
3rd Cold. Gds	-	-	2	2
...	-	-	2	2
1st Irish	-	-	-	1
R.E. McC ott & 4d Amb	1	-	-	-
1st M. R.R. att 2nd Signal	-	-	1	-
R.E. 2nd Signals	1	-	-	-
2nd H.R.J.	-	-	6	-
9th H.R.J.	-	-	7	-
2nd Lanc. Fusil	-	-	7	1
1st Queens	-	-	1	-
R.G.A. 7th M.B.	-	-	1	-
R.F.A. 41st Bde.	-	1	2	-
" 44th "	-	-	-	-
	2	2	25	5
Other Divns				
R.G.A. 5th Siege B	-	-	1	-
" 11th "	-	-	2	-
" 35th H.B.	-	-	1	-
	-	-	4	-

To Duty:
	Sick	Wnd
1st Herts	1	-
2nd O & Bucks	1	-
1st Queens	1	-
9th H.R.J.	1	-
	4	-

To m/Con.Coy.
	Sick	Wnd
2nd Green Gds.	1	-
3rd Cold "	1	-
2nd O & Bucks	2	-
2nd H.R.J.	2	-
2nd Lanc	1	-
7th Kings	1	-
1st Bucks	1	-
	9	-

Caries Dentine 11

	Sick	Wnd
Admitted Officers	2	2
" Other Rks	29	5
Evacd Officers	2	2
" Other Rks	19	6
Remaing Officers	-	1
" Other Rks	59	6

Evacd By M.A.C.
	sick	wnd
Officers	2	2
Other rks	19	6

To Duty
Other Rks	4	-

To 2nd Div Con Coy | 9 | -

Admitted Officers

2nd Green. Gds (Bde Staff) (T.F.) — Capt. G.L. DERRIMAN — Shell Wnd Right arm & leg.

Chaplain Dept (att No 4 Fd Amb) — Rev. F. de W. LUSHINGTON — V.D.H.

R.E. 2nd Signal Co — M/Lt. H.C. CRONE — N.Y.D. Pyrexia

R.F.A. 41st Bde. — Lieut H.C. CORY — Shell Wound Shrapnel arm & leg

J.J. O'Keeffe
Capt RAMC
O.C. No 4 Field Amb.

WMS 2nd Div.
21/7/15

Army Form C. 2118

WAR DIARY
or
INTELLIGENCE SUMMARY

(Erase heading not required.)

Instructions regarding War Diaries and Intelligence Summaries are contained in F. S. Regs., Part II. and the Staff Manual respectively. Title Pages will be prepared in manuscript.

Place	Date	Hour	Summary of Events and Information	Remarks and references to Appendices
BETHUNE	21/7/15		Number of Casualties. Officers 4 Other Ranks 34	
			Evacuated by 7 M.A.C. " " " 25	
			Discharged to duty , Nil , " " 4	
			" Conv. Coy. , Nil , " " 7	
"	22/7/15		Lieut. Cockcroft, R.A.M.C. Proceeded for temporary duty with 36th Bde. R.F.A.	
			No. 8859 Cpl Lucas, R.A.M.C. Proceeded on leave to England.	
			As a result of severe shelling of the town, which commenced about 6 p.m. 19 wounded were admitted; 2 of these cases died shortly after admission.	PK4
			The D.A.D.M.S. visited the hospital to obtain particulars of these casualties.	
			Lieut. Sherman R.A.M.C. arrived for duty from No. 6 Fd. Ambce. and proceeded forthwith to the Advanced Dressing Station in relief of Lieut. Andrews, R.A.M.C. who proceeded as M.O. to 1st. Kings (Liverpool) Regt.	
			1 N.C.O. and 6 men joined as reinforcements from the Base.	
			Number of Casualties. Officers 2 Other Ranks 44.	
			Evacuated by No. 7. M.A.C. " 1 " " 18.	
			Discharged to duty " Nil " " 8	
			" Conv. Coy. " Nil " " 7.	
"	23/7/15		D.A.D.M.S. twice visited the Dressing Station. Commanding officer returned from leave.	
			Number of Casualties. Officers 1 Other Ranks 18	
			Evacuated by No. 7. M.A.C. " Nil " " 8	
			Discharged to duty " 1 " " 15	
			" Conv. Coy. " Nil " " 6.	

No. 4 Field Ambulance
Sick & wounded admitted, by Unit, during
24 hours ended 9 am. 22/7/15.

2nd Div. Units	Officers		Other Ranks	
	Sick	Wnd	Sick	Wnd
2nd Cold. Gds.	-	-	4	-
3rd " "	1	-	2	1
1st Irish "	-	-	2	1
1st Herts	-	-	1	-
2nd Innis. Fusil.	-	-	1	-
9th H.L.I.	-	-	1	-
2nd Ox't & Bucks	-	-	4	-
2nd H.L.I.	-	1	5	-
1st Queens	-	1	-	-
12t K.R.R.	-	-	4	-
7th Kings	-	1	-	-
2nd Workers	-	-	-	1
R.E. 5th Co.	-	-	1	-
R.F.A. 47th Batt.	-	-	1	-
" 56th	-	-	1	-
	1	2	26	3

To Duty:		Sick	Wnd
3rd Cold. Gds.		1	1
1st Herts		2	-
2nd Ox & Bucks		1	-
A. Cycle Corps		1	-
Rame ass't. med'nnis		1	-
R.G.A 9th Siege B.		1	-
" 6th Transp't		-	-
9th H.L.I.		1	-
		9	1

To 2nd Div. Con. Co.
2nd Cold. Gds.   1   -

Other Divns.

	Officers		Other Ranks	
	Sick	Wnd	Sick	Wnd
A.S.C. M.T. 1st Div.				
70 Amb. workshop	-	-	1	-
R.E. 31st Fortress Co	-	-	1	1
" 176th Co	-	-	1	-
RGA 9th Siege B.	-	-	1	-
" 25th Batt.	-	-	1	-
	-	-	5	1

Evac'd by M.A.C.	Sick	Wnd.
Officers	-	1
Other Rks	13	2
To Duty		
Other Rks	9	1
To 2nd Div. Con. Coy		
Other Rks	1	-

		Sick	Wnd
Admitted Officers		1	2
" Other Rks		31	4
Evac'd Officers		-	1
" Other Rks		13	2
Remaining Officers		1	2
" Other Rks		27	7

J. O'Keefe
Capt RAMC
O/C No 4 Field Ambce

DMS 2nd Divn.
22/7/15

No 4 Field Ambulance
Sick & wounded admitted by units during
24 hours ended 9 am 23/7/15

2nd Div. Units	Officers		Other ranks	
	Sick	Wnd	Sick	Wnd
2nd Grenr. Gds	-	-	2	-
2nd Cold. "	-	-	1	-
1st Irish "	-	-	1	1
1st Herts	-	-	2	1
2nd Oxf & Bucks	-	-	2	6
2nd H.L.I.	-	-	3	-
7th H.L.I.	-	-	2	-
2nd Worcesters	-	-	1	1
2nd Innis. Fus.	-	-	3	13
R.E. 2nd Signals	-	-	1	2
" 11th Co	-	-	1	-
R.A.M.C. att 1st Kings	1	-	-	-
	1	-	19	23

Other Divns
1st Cold. Guards	-	1	-	1
R.E. 31st Fortress Co	-	-	1	-
	-	1	1	1

To Duty:
	Sick	Wnd
2nd Cold Gds	0	1
1st Irish "	3	-
7th Kings	1	-
2nd Innis	2	-
	7	1

To 2nd Div. Con. Coy.
2nd Gren Gds	1	-
7th Kings	1	-
2nd Innis Fus	2	-
2nd O.B.B.	1	-
2nd H.L.I.	1	-
R.F.A. 30th Batt.	1	-
	7	-

Evac'd by M.A.C.
	Sick	Wnd
Officers	-	1
Other ranks	1	17

To Duty
| Other ranks | 7 | 1 |

2nd Div. Con Coy
| Other ranks | 7 | - |

Deaths Other R's — 3

	Sick	Wnd
Admitted Officers	1	1
" Other R's	20	24
Evac'd Officers	-	1
" Other R's	1	17
Remain'g Officers	2	2
" Other R's	22	10

Admitted Officers
1st Coldstream Gds 2nd Lieut. F.M. FISHER — Cont Wound L. leg
R.A.M.C. att 1st Kings Lieut. S.F.M. CESARI N.Y.D. Fever

Evacuated Sick other ranks
2nd Innis. Fusil. 1.

J. J. O'Ruff
Capt R.A.M.C.
O/C No 4 F.A.

A.D.M.S. 2nd Division
23/7/15

No. 4 Field Ambulance

Sick & wounded admitted, by Units, during 24 hours ended 9 a.m. 24/7/15

2nd Div. Units	Officers		Other Rks	
	Sick	Wnd	Sick	Wnd
1st Herts	-	-	2	-
2nd H.L.I.	-	-	3	-
2nd Oxf & Bucks	-	-	3	1
2nd Innis. Fusil.	1	-	2	-
2nd Worcesters	-	-	2	-
South Irish Horse	-	-	2	-
R.E. 11th Co.	-	-	1	-
R.A.M.C. (75) 2/1 R.E. } 1 East Ang. }	-	-	1	-
R.F.A. 9th Batt	-	-	1	-
R.G.A. 7th mount. By	-	-	1	1
	1	-	15	2

(* Indian Soldier)

Other Divns

1st King's att. 176th } Co. R.E. }	-	-	-	1
				1

To Duty:	Officers		Other Rks	
	Sick	Wnd	Sick	Wnd
3rd Colds. Gds.	1	-	-	-
2nd " "	-	-	1	-
2nd Grem. Gds.	-	-	1	-
2nd H.L.I.	-	-	5	-
9th "	-	-	1	-
2nd Worcesters	-	-	1	-
10th KRR & 2nd Sig. nals	-	-	1	-
R.E. 2nd Signals	-	-	1	1
2nd Innis. + cas.	-	-	1	-
1st Herts	-	-	1	-
R.G.A. 20th H.B.	-	-	1	-
Total	1	-	13	2

2nd Div. Con. Coy	-	-	1	-
2nd Gren. Gds.	-	-	1	-
2nd H.L.I.	-	-	2	-
9th "	-	-	1	-
2nd Innis + cas.	-	-	1	-
2nd Oxf/Bucks	-	-	1	-
Total	-	-	6	-

Evacuated by M.A.C.   Sick Wnd
  Officers   0   0
  Other ranks 6   2
  Indian Soldier 0 1

To Duty
  Officers   1   0
  Other ranks 13   2

To 2nd Div. Con. Coy
  Other ranks 6   0

Admitted   Sick Wnd
  Officers   1   0
  Other ranks } 15   3
  (including 1 Indian wounded)

Evacuated
  Officers   0   0
  Other ranks (including 1 wnd. Indian) 6 3

Remaining
  Officers   2   2
  Other Rks   62   8

Officer Admitted

2nd Innis. Fusil. Capt & Adjt. C.A.M. ALEXANDER — dislocation R. clavicle

P.H. Lloyd Jones
Major R.A.M.C.
O/C No 4 Field Ambce

aldws 2nd Wivn.
24/7/15

Army Form C. 2118

WAR DIARY
or
INTELLIGENCE SUMMARY
(Erase heading not required.)

Instructions regarding War Diaries and Intelligence Summaries are contained in F. S. Regs., Part II. and the Staff Manual respectively. Title Pages will be prepared in manuscript.

Place	Date	Hour	Summary of Events and Information	Remarks and references to Appendices
BETHUNE	24/7/15		The A.D.M.S. 1st Corps inspected the Dressing Station. Number of Casualties officers 1 other Ranks 52 Evacuated by No.7 M.A.C. " " 18 " by Barge " Nil " 2. " " " " Nil " 8. Discharged to duty " Nil " 4. " " Conv. Coy. " Nil " -	
"	25/7/15		A.D.M.S. 2nd Div: inspected the Dressing Station. The Commanding Officer inspected the Advanced Dressing Stations at BEUVRY and No.1 Haney Street. Number of Casualties Officers 1 other Ranks 28 Evacuated by No 7 M.A.C. " 1 " 18 Discharged to duty " Nil " 9 " - Convalescent Coy. - Nil " 23.	OK.Y.
"	26/7/15		Took over field as a farm about 1½ miles West of the town for slight cases of sickness and wounded. Capt J.J. O'Keeffe RAMC. to take charge of this. The field was taken over and opened in the afternoon. The cases being treated under canvas. S/Sgt Moon, RAMC. and 2 other N.C.O's, 2 Cooks, 4 nursing and 4 General Duty orderlies, 2 Sanitary Squad, 2 Police and 1 cycle orderly men left this for duty. 3 A.S.C.(M.T.) and 2 A.S.C.(HT) No. 3611 Pte Garruthy, RAMC. proceeded to Base Depot for his discharge.	P

1875 Wt. W593/826 1,000,000 4/15 J.B.C. & A. A.D.S.S./Forms/C. 2118.

No 4 Field Ambulance
Sick & Wounded admitted, by Units,
during 24 hours ending 25/7/15.

2nd Div. Units	Officers		Other ranks				
	sick	wnd	sick	wnd			
2nd Gren. Gds.	-	-	1	1	To Duty:	sick	wnd
3rd Cold.	-	-	2	-	Other R.Rs:-		
1st Herts	-	-	3	-			
2nd Oxf & Bucks	-	-	2	1	1st Irish Gd	1	-
2nd Worcesters	-	-	2	-	2nd Oxf & Bucks	2	-
2nd High. L.I.	-	-	-	11	2nd R. Innis. Fus	-	1
1st Queens	-	-	4	1	R.G.A. 9th S.B.	1	-
5th Kings	-	-	-	-	- 11th -	1	-
1st K.R.Rif.C.	-	-	2	-	- 35th N.B.	1	-
2nd R. Innis. Fus	-	-	-	1			
1st R. Berks R.	-	-	1	-			
A.S.C.M.T. att 4 Fd Amb.	-	-	1	-	Total	7	1
R.E. 5th Coy	-	-	1	-			
R.F.A. 17th Batt	-	-	1	1			
- 70th -	-	-	1	-			
R.F.A. 9th siege Bty	-	-	2	-	2nd Div. Cav. Coy		
- 2nd Heavy -	-	-	1	-	Other R.Rs:-		
	-	-	30	17	2nd Oxf & Bucks	1	-
					2nd R. Innis. Fus	1	-
Other Divns					2nd High. L.I.	1	-
A.S.C.M.T. att 12th Div} Field Amb. W.W.}	-	-	1	-	R. Flying Corps	1	-
					Total	4	-
1st Manchesters R. att. 176th Co. R.E.	1	-	-	-			
A. Ord. Corps att. R.G.A. 11th Siege Bty	-	-	1	-			
R.F.A. 40th How.Bde	-	-	1	-			
2nd S. Staffs R. att } 176th Co. R.E. }	-	-	1	-			
176th Co R.E.	-	-	1	-			
	1	-	5	-			

C.T.O.

2.

Evacuated by M.A.C.	Sick	Wnd.	Admitted	Sick	Wnd
Officers	–	–	Officers	1	–
Other ranks	10	8	Other Rks	35	17
Evac'd by M.A.C. by Barge			Evacuated		
Other ranks	–	2	Officers	–	–
To Duty			Other Rks	10	10
Other ranks	7	1	Remaining		
2nd Div. Com. Coy			Officers	3	2
Other ranks	4	–	Other Rks	76	14

Officer Admitted

1st Manchester Regt } Lieut. J.R.G. GWYTHER N.Y.D. fever
att. R.E. 176th Co }

P.A. Lloyd Jones

A.D.M.S. 2nd Div'n   Major R.A.M.C.
25/7/15   O.C. No 4 Field Amb'ce.

No 4 Field Ambulance.
Sick & wounded admitted, by Units, during
24 hours ended 26th July 1915.

2nd Div. Units	Officers		Other Ranks	
	Sick	Wound	Sick	Wound
2nd Grew. Guards	-	-	1	-
2nd Cold. "	-	-	1	-
1st Herts	-	-	1	-
Same 4 Fd Amb	-	-	1	-
1st K.R.Rif.C.	-	1	-	-
2nd Worcesters	-	-	-	1
2nd High. L.I.	-	-	4	1
9th do	-	-	1	3
2nd Oxf. & Bucks	-	-	1	1
R.E. 11th Field Co	-	-	1	-
R.F.A. 70th Bty.	-	-	2	-
R.G.A. 4th Mount Bty	-	-	1	-
	-	1	14	6

Other Div.n				
R.E. 170th Co.	-	-	1	3
Scots Guards att.} R.E. 170th Co. }	-	-	-	1
R.F.A. 30th Bty	-	-	1	-
Royal Flying C.	-	-	1	-
3rd Queens	-	-	-	1
	-	-	3	5

To Duty:	Other Ranks Sick	Other Ranks Wnd
2nd H.L.I.	4	-
2nd Oxf & Bucks	2	-
South Irish Horse	1	-
R.E. 5th Co	1	-
Army Ord. Corps	1	-
	9	-

To 2nd Div. Con. Coy		
1st Irish Rts	-	1
R.A.M.C. 4 Fd Amb	1	2
2nd Oxf & Bucks	1	-
2nd High. L.I.	7	1
2nd Worcesters	2	-
2nd R. Innis. Fus.	2	-
1st R. Berks. R.	1	-
R.F.A. 56th Bty.	1	-
" 9th "	1	-
A.S.C. M.T. att 1st Div. 7 Amb. N.M.	1	-
	19	4

	Sick	Wnd
Evacuated by M.A.C.		
Officers	-	1
Other Rks	13	5
Evac by Barge		
Other Ranks	-	1
To Duty " "	9	-
2nd Div. Con. Coy Other Ranks	19	4
Deaths " "	-	2

	Sick	Wnd
Admitted Officers	-	1
" Other Rks	17	11
Evac. Officers	-	1
" Other Rks	13	6
Remaining Officers	3	2
" Other Rks	52	13

Officers Admitted
1st Kings Royal Rif.C. 2nd Lt. G.T. DEWHURST

P.A. Lloyd Jones
Major RAMC
O.C. No 4 Field Ambce.

D.M.S. 2nd Division
26/7/15

No. 4 Field Ambulance
Sick & wounded admitted by Unit
during 24 hours ended 9 a.m. 27/7/15

2nd Divn Unit	Officers		Other Rks			S.	W.
	Sick	Wnd	Sick	Wnd			
2nd Green Gds	-	-	3	-	To 2nd Div. Cav. Coy.		
3rd Cold. Gds	-	-	2	-			
1st Irish Gds	-	-	3	-	1st Herts	2	-
1st Herts	-	-	1	-	2nd Oxf & Bucks	1	1
R.A.M.C. No 4 F.Amb	-	-	-	1	9th High. L.I.	-	1
2nd Worcesters	-	-	2	-	2nd High. L.I.	3	1
2nd High. L.I.	-	-	-	1	2nd Worcesters	1	-
1st Queens	-	-	-	2	R.F.A. 9th Bty	1	-
S. Irish Horse	-	-	1	-	R.E. 170th Co	-	2
1st Kings	-	-	-	-		8	4
1st Shropshire L.I.	1	1	-	-			
att 1st Kings							
	1	1	12	4	To Duty		
Other Divns					2nd Oxf & Bucks	1	-
R.Flying Corps	-	-	2	-			
R.E. 176th Co.	-	-	1	1			
	-	-	3	1			

Evac.d by M.A.C.	Sick	Wnd			Sick	Wnd
Officers	1	-	Admitted Officers		1	1
Other Rks	5	2	" Other Rks		15	5
To Duty Other Rks	1	-	Evac.d Officers		1	-
To 2nd Div. Cav. Coy. Other Rks	8	4	" Other Rks		5	2
			Remaining Officers		3	3
			Other Rks		53	12

Officers Admitted

1st Kings 2nd Lieut. H.E. HASELHURST N.Y.D. Fever
1st Shropshire L.I. 2nd Lt. J.K. MYLIUS Shell wound left
att. 1st Kings.   arm.

P. Ashby Jones

A.D.M.S. 2nd Division   Major R.A.M.C.
    27/7/15   O.C. No 4 Field Amb.

Army Form C. 2118

WAR DIARY
or
INTELLIGENCE SUMMARY
(Erase heading not required.)

Instructions regarding War Diaries and Intelligence Summaries are contained in F. S. Regs., Part II. and the Staff Manual respectively. Title Pages will be prepared in manuscript.

Place	Date	Hour	Summary of Events and Information	Remarks and references to Appendices
BETHUNE	26/7/15		No. 55407 Pte Draper, RAMC evacuated to Base with wound contracted. Medical Board was held on Lieut Allison, A.L. Sect's Batty, R.G.A. a candidate for commission in the Regular Forces. He was found medically fit. Number of Casualties: Officers 2 : Other Ranks 20. Evacuated by No. 7 M.A.C. officers 1 " " 7. Discharged to duty " nil " " 1. " " Conv. Coy " nil " " 12.	OK.
"	27/7/15		Medical Boards on Lieuts Weeks, 1st Irish Guards and Cpl. Parrington, 3rd Coldstream Guards, were held, both candidates for Commissions in the Regular Forces. Capt. McCullagh, RAMC returned from leave. Revd. F. Morley, and No. 19711 Sgt. S.B. Horshead proceeded on leave. Number of Casualties: officers 2 other ranks 15. Evacuated by M.A.C. " 1 " " 8. Discharged to duty " nil " " 4. " " Conv. Coy " nil " " 1.	
"	28/7/15		A.D.M.S. visited the Dressing Station. Number of Casualties officers 4 other Ranks 19. Evacuated by No 7 M.A.C " 1 " " 8. Discharged to duty " nil " " nil " " Conv. Coy " nil " " 1.	

No 4 Field Ambulance.
Sick & wounded admitted by units during
24 hours ended 9 am. 28/7/15

2nd Divn Units	Officers		Other Ranks	
	Sick	Wnd	Sick	Wnd
2nd Green Gds	-	-	1	-
3rd Cold	-	-	2	-
1st Irish	-	-	2	-
2th Kings	1	-	1	-
2nd High L.I.	-	-	1	1
9th "	1	-	2	-
2nd Worcesters	-	-	1	-
South Irish Horse	-	-	1	-
R.F.A. 17th Bty	-	-	1	-
" 20th Bty	-	-	1	-
	2	-	11	1

To Duty:	sick	wnd
R.E. 9th M.B.	1	-
R.E. 5th Co	1	-
2nd Oxf & Bucks	1	-
ASC M.T. 1st Divn workshop U.	1	-
	4	-
2 2nd Div Cav Coy		
2nd H.L.I.	1	-

Other Divisions.

	Officers		Other Ranks	
	Sick	Wnd	Sick	Wnd
R.F.A. 40th Bty	-	-	1	-
R.G.A. 24th	-	-	-	1
2nd S.Staff. 6st	-	-	1	-
76th Co.?	-	-	1	-
	-	-	2	1

Influenza 6

Evacs by M.A.C.	sick	wnd
Officers	-	-
Other ranks	7	1
To Duty:		
Other ranks	4	-
To 2nd Div Cav Coy		
Other ranks	1	-

Admitted	sick	wnd
Officers	2	-
Other Rks	13	2
Evacs Officers	-	1
Other Rks	7	1
Remaining Officers	5	2
" at M.D.S. Other Rks	36	10
" " Moncove Convt Camp Other Rks	18	3

Officers Admitted
9th High L.I. Lieut. E.J. WHITSON Conjunctivitis
7th Kings Shrops Lt. T.G. WILLIAMS Dysentery.

M.C. 2nd Divn.
28/7/15

Major RAMC
O.C. No 4 Field Ambulance

No 4 Field Ambulance
Sick & wounded admitted, by units,
during 24 hours ended 9 a.m. 29.7.15.

2nd Divl Units	Officers		Other ranks		
	sick	wnd	sick	wnd	
2nd Gren Gds	-	-	2	-	
1st Herts	-	-	3	-	
South Irish Horse	-	-	1	-	
2nd Worcesters	-	-	2	-	
2nd South Staffs	-	1	-	-	
3rd Black Watch } att. 2nd H.L.I & K.O.S.B }	-	1	-	-	
2nd High. L.I.	-	-	-	1	
1st Queens	-	-	-	1	
R.F.A. 41st Bde	-	-	1	-	
R.E. 1st East Ang.	1	-	-	-	
	1	2	9	2	
Other Divns					
Royal Flying Corps	-	-	1	-	
R.E. 31st Fortress Co	-	-	2	-	
A.S.C. 11th Anti Aircraft Coy.	-	-	1	-	
R.G.A. 20th H.Bty.	-	-	1	-	
R.F.A. 30th Bty	-	-	1	-	
2nd Gordon Hdrs.	-	-	1	-	
1st Royal Marine Art:	-	-	-	1	
R.E. 176th Co	-	1	-	-	
	-	1	7	1	

Officers Admitted
Lieut. A.S.R. HUGHES 2nd S.Staffs Scalp wnd eye.
Lieut. E. CORIS-SCOTT R.E. 176th Co stiff Bruise & arm.
Lieut. R.A. DOUGLAS 3rd B. Watch att. 2nd High.R.I. Bomb L. leg & knee.
Lieut. A.M. MATTHEWS R.E. 1st East Ang. 2nd H.L.I. Pyrexia

Prevailing Disease Nil

Evacd by M.A.C.	sick	wnd.
Officers	-	1
Other ranks	6	2
To Duty	-	-
To 2nd Div. Con Coy	1	-
Other ranks		
To MONDORE from M.D.S.		
Other ranks 16		

To 2nd Div. Con. Coy.
1st Irish Gds. other rank 1.

Admitted		sick	wnd
"	Officers	1	3
"	Other Rks	16	3
Evacd	Officers	-	1
"	Other rks	6	2
Remaing	Officers	1	4
"	Other Rks at Main Dressing Stn	29	9
"	Other ranks at MONDORE	34	5
	Total Other ranks remaining	63	14

A.D.M.S. 2nd Division
29.7.15

P.H. Lloyd Jones
Major R.A.M.C.
O.C. No 4 Field Amb.

WAR DIARY or INTELLIGENCE SUMMARY

Army Form C. 2118

Place	Date	Hour	Summary of Events and Information	Remarks and references to Appendices
BETHUNE	29/7/15		Received orders to hand over the Advanced Dressing Station at No. 1 Harley Street and also the Buildings at BEUVRY to No 6 Field Ambulance, and take over from them the evacuation of the line just North of Canal and Advanced Dressing Station at LE PREOL. Also to have a M.O. and a Nurse personnel working in conjunction with a Field Ambulance of the 9th. Divn. at MARAIS F.10.d. Capt. McCullagh to send out to complete the details for the collection of wounded in this area at MARAIS. No. 864 Pte Toy (or D.) Rhyne rejoined from Hospital Base.	
			Number of Casualties, Officers Nil. Other Ranks 25. Evacuated by No. 7 M.A.C. " 1 " " 15. " " Conv. Coy. " Nil " " 6. Discharged to duty Nil Nil	
"	30/7/15		A.D.M.S. 2nd Divn. visited the Dressing Station yesterday evening. Commanding officer visited LE PREOL and also the Advanced Dressing Station of the Field Ambulance of 9th. Divn. near MARAIS. I thought the times of evacuations were not convenient, and decided to make one line if possible. Capt. McCullagh is investigating this.	
			Number of Casualties - Officers 2 Other Ranks 16. Evacuated by M.A.C. " Nil " " 11. " " " " Nil " " 6. Discharged to duty Nil " " 10. " " Conv. Coy.	

No 4 Field Ambulance
Sick & Wounded admitted by Units
during 24 hours ended 9 am. 30/7/15

2nd Div Units	Officers		Other ranks	
	Sick	Wnd	Sick	Wnd.
2nd Grew. Gds.	-	-	3	1
3rd Cold. Gds.	-	-	2	-
1st Irish "	-	-	2	-
1st Herts	-	-	2	-
2nd Worcesters	-	-	3	-
1st Queens	-	-	-	6
9th High. L.I.	-	-	1	-
2nd S. Staffs	-	-	1	-
2nd Oxf & Bucks	-	-	-	1
R.E. 11th Field Co	-	-	1	-
2nd High L.I.	-	-	1	-
1st King	-	-	1	-
	-	-	17	7

Other Divns

Royal Naval Art. S. - - - 1

Prevailing Diseases nil

		S.	W.
Evac: by 7 M.A.C	S.	W	Admitted Officers	-	-
Officers	-	1	" Other Rks	17	8
Other ranks	9	6	Evacuated Officers	-	1
To Duty	-	-	" Other Rks	9	6
To 2nd Div. Con. Coy	6	-	Remaining Officers	-	3
Death		1	" Other Ranks at M.D.S. 32 / 5
			" ... at mondore 33 / 10	65	15

To 2nd Div. Con. Coy
1st Herts other rank sick 1.

P. A. Lloyd Jones.

A.D.M.S. 2nd Divn.   Major R.A.M.C.
30/7/15   O.C. No 4 Field Amb.

Army Form C. 2118

WAR DIARY
or
INTELLIGENCE SUMMARY
(Erase heading not required.)

Instructions regarding War Diaries and Intelligence Summaries are contained in F. S. Regs., Part II. and the Staff Manual respectively. Title Pages will be prepared in manuscript.

Place	Date	Hour	Summary of Events and Information	Remarks and references to Appendices
BETHUNE	31/7/15		Farm with very good cellar taken about 300 yards on a road running West from "Windy Corner". From here, in fine weather, cases can be evacuated over "WESTMINSTER" Bridge and by road parallel to South Bank of Canal. Permission is being tried for us to take motor Ambulances along the canal bank either on North or South banks (N. Bank, difficult). A small personnel will be left at the dressing station at Canal Junction. Evacuation from Regiment at Rest Posts. The three aid posts near Windy Corner are easy to work. Cases from the battalion on the top of the line are to be kept in dug outs in the trenches till night and then removed by hand, down a communication trench to "YELLOW ROAD", and thence by wheeled stretcher along track to the Dressing Station. The track can be repaired locally. Telephone installed from A.D.S. to this Aid post. The A.D. 2nd Div. visited the Dressing Station to see Lieut. Col. STEAVENSON 1st Kings (L'pool) Regt. attached with N.V.D. Rectum. Divnl. decided to send him to No.1 Casualty Clearing Station CHOCQUES for examination. Lieut EARP, O.C. 7B. Ambce. Workshop Unit, walked proposed line of evacuation with officer commanding and gave expert opinion about the road North of Canal between WESTMINSTER BRIDGE and Canal junction. He stated that it might be used by motor Ambulances with safety provided that in the day time	(PKG) PKG

1875 Wt. W593/826 1,000,000 4/15 J.B.C. & A. A.D.S.S./Forms/C. 2118.

Army Form C. 2118

WAR DIARY
or
INTELLIGENCE SUMMARY
(Erase heading not required.)

Instructions regarding War Diaries and Intelligence Summaries are contained in F.S. Regs, Part II and the Staff Manual respectively. Title Pages will be prepared in manuscript.

Place	Date	Hour	Summary of Events and Information	Remarks and references to Appendices
BETHUNE	31/7/15		They did not exceed the pace of 5 m.p.h. and at night they went at the same pace and had a man walking in front of each motor Ambulance. If the North Bank of the canal is used covered lights should be employed on pontoon bridge at Caine junction. Number of Casualties- Officers 1 Other Ranks 27. Evacuated by M.A.C. " 1 " " 3. " Barge " Nil " " 1. " discharged to duty " Nil " " 7. Received information that bridge at PONT FIXE was now repaired after recent shelling and could now take 3 tons weight. Have stated to do evacuation by this route at present. The 1st Division Staff have had to refuse permission from the HARLEY STREET and also HARLEY STREET the Canal bank roads. The railway crossing at WESTMINSTER BRIDGE is being repaired and is suitable for motor Ambulances the new bridge from the — to CANAL JUNCTION is to be referred by 1st CORPS Submission will be conducted by this route when these are finished. This route is at present impossible in wet weather.	PM4.

No. 4 Field Ambulance.

Sick and Wnd admitted by units during 24 hours ended 7am 2/7/15.

	Officers		Other Rks	
	Sick	Wnd	Sick	Wnd
2nd Div. Amn.	–	–	–	–
2nd Gren. Gds.	–	–	1	–
Total	–	–	1	–

Comm. Coy.
R.G.A. 111th Batt. 1.
2nd Gren. Gds. 1.

Evac'd M.A.C.
Officers Nil
Other Rks 1.
To Duty Nil
Conv. Coy.
Other Rks 2.

	Sick	Wnd
Admitted Officers	–	–
Other Rks	1	–
Evac'd Officers	–	–
Other Rks	1	–
Remng Officers	1	–
Other Rks	7	2.

Evac'd SICK.
2nd Gren. Gds. 1.

P.A. Lloyd Jones
Capt. R.A.M.C.
OC. No. 4 Fd. Ambce.

A.D.M.S. 2nd Div.
2/7/15.

No 4 Field Ambulance
Sick + wnd admitted by Units, during 24 hours
ended 9 am 3/7/15

	Officers		Other ranks	
	Sick	Wnd.	Sick	Wnd.
	–	–	–	–
	–	–	–	–

			Sick	Wnd.
Evacuated to MAC		Admitted Officers	–	–
Officers nil		" Other rks	–	–
Other rks –				
To Duty		Evacuated Officers	–	–
Officers 1		" Other rks	–	–
Other rks nil		Remng. Officers	–	–
Con. Coy		" Other rks	7	2
Other ranks nil				

P. A. Lloyd Jones.
Capt R.A.M.C.
O.C. No 4 Field Ambce

A.D.M.S. 2nd Div.
3/7/15

No 4 Field Ambulance
Sick + wnd admitted, by units, during 24 hours
ended 9 a.m. 4/7/15

2nd Div Units	Officers		Other Ranks	
	Sick	wnd	Sick	wnd
2nd Colo. Coy.	-	-	3	-
A.S.C. No 2 Coy.	-	-	1	-
	-	-	4	-

Evac? M.A.C.   Admitted Officers   Sick wnd
Officers nil   " Other ranks 4   -
Other rks 1   Evac? Officers   -   -
To Duty nil   " Other rks 1   -
Con. Coy   Remaining Officers -   -
Other Rks 1   " Other rks. 9   2

        Evac? Sick
        2nd Colo. Coy.   1

                                        P.H. C?? Jones.
   A.D.M.S.   Capt. R.A.M.C.
    2nd Div.   O.C. No 4 Fd Amb.
    4/7/15

No 4 Field Ambulance

Sick & Wounded admitted by Units during 24 hours ended 9 am 31/7/15

2nd Divn Unit	Officers		Other ranks	
	Sick	Wnd	Sick	Wnd
2nd Grendr Gds	-	-	1	-
2nd Coldm Gds	-	-	1	1
3rd " "	-	-	-	1
1st Irish	-	-	-	4
R.A.M.C. No 5 Fd Amb	-	-	1	-
1st Herts	-	-	1	-
1st Kings	2	-	-	-
	2	-	4	6

Other Divns				
1st Cold Gds	-	-	1	-
R. Welsh Fus	-	-	1	-
R.F.A. 30th Bty	-	-	2	-
" 21st Anti aircraft	-	-	1	-
R.G.A. 26th Bty	-	-	1	-
	-	-	6	-

To 2nd Div. Con. Coy — Other ranks — S W
- 2nd Grenr Gds — 1 —
- 2nd Coldm " — 1 —
- 3rd " " — 2 —
- 1st Herts — 1 —
- 2nd Worcesters — 1 —
- 9th High L.I. — 1 —
- R.E. 178th Co — 1 —
- R. Flying Corps — 2 —
- Total — 10 —

To Duty. Other ranks
- 9th High L.I. — 1 —
- R.G.A. 35th Bty — 1 —
- 2nd High L.I. — 1 2
- 1st Queens — — 1
- Total — 3 3

Cases Dental — 5

	S	W
Evac: by M.A.C.		
Officer	-	-
Other ranks	9	2
To 2nd Div. Con. Coy		
Other ranks	10	-
To Duty		
Other ranks	3	3

	S	W
Admitted Officers	2	-
Other ranks	10	1
Evacuated Officers	-	-
Other ranks	9	2
Remaining Officers	8	3
Other ranks at M.D.S.	29	9
" " " at Minime	24	7
	53	16

Officers Admitted

1st Kings (Pools) Lt. Col. STEAVENSON, C.T. N.Y.D. Fistula
1st King 2nd Lt. HUTSON, F.R.

R. A. Lloyd Jones
Major R.A.M.C.
O.C. No 4 Field Amb.

A.D.M.S. 2nd Division
31/7/15

No. 4 Field Ambulance

Sick & wounded admitted, by unit, during 24 hours ended 9 am. 5/7/15

2nd Div. Units	Officers		Other Ranks	
	Sick	Wnd	Sick	Wnd
2nd Cold. Gds	–	–	1	–
RAMC 4 F. Amb	–	–	2	–
	–	–	3	–

	Sick	Wnd
Evac'd M.A.C.		
Officers nil	Admitted Officers	–	–
Other rks 4	" Other rks	3	–
To Duty nil	Evac'd Officers	–	–
Con Coy nil	" Other rks	4	–
	Remaining Officers	–	–
	Other rks	8	2

Evacuated Sick
2nd Cold. Guards 3
R.A.M.C. No 4 7. a 1

A.D.M.S.
2nd Div.
5/7/15.

P. H. Lloyd Jones
Capt. R.A.M.C.
O.C. No 4 F. Amb.

www.ingramcontent.com/pod-product-compliance
Lightning Source LLC
Chambersburg PA
CBHW081437160426
43193CB00013B/2305